IT'S MY BELIEF

It's My Belief

JAMES MARTIN

THE SAINT ANDREW PRESS
EDINBURGH

First published in 1991 by
THE SAINT ANDREW PRESS
121 George Street, Edinburgh EH2 4YN

ISBN 0 7152 0648 6

British Library Cataloguing in Publication Data
Martin, James 1921-
It's my belief.
1. Jesus Christ. Historicity
I. Title
232.908

ISBN 0-7152-0648-6

This book has been set in 11/12.5 pt Times Roman.

Printed and bound by Billing & Sons Ltd, Worcester

Contents

Introduction

I RECALL attending a meeting which was vigorously and somewhat agonisingly discussing the priorities of Christian Mission for our day, when suddenly one of the committee members burst out with some vehemence, 'The chief trouble today is that so many people simply do not think that what we preach is true'.

Christians in the latter part of the twentieth century have spent a considerable amount of time and energy attempting to make the Gospel message patently and persuasively relevant. Probably just as much time and as much energy have been employed in the endeavours to present that message in a persuasively attractive way.

In face of the considerable apathy and disinterest shown towards the Church and the Gospel it seeks to proclaim, such efforts are undoubtedly of great importance and much to be commended. It may not always be the case, however, when presentation of the Gospel message appears to be having little success in winning converts, that the reason for failure is to be found in either of the areas mentioned.

Just as often—perhaps more often as my fellow committee member insisted—the reason may be that our hearers are sceptical about the truth of what we are proclaiming. This is a great pity because—I firmly believe —the fundamentals of the Christian Faith have a solid historical base. There is very good reason to believe in the Christian Gospel and, in my opinion at least, belief beats unbelief and beats it hands down.

This is not to suggest that the Christian Faith or its

component parts can be *proved* to be true beyond any shadow of doubt. Faith must always be faith. When it becomes sight or certain knowledge then, *ipso facto*, it is no longer faith. At the same time, this does not mean that faith must be, or even *may* be, unreasonable; still less does it mean that it should be anti-reason.

Christian Faith is never meant to be an unreasonable thing. A schoolboy once defined faith as 'believing in something which you know isn't true'. A number of people think like this about the Christian Faith: that being a Christian means holding grimly, sometimes desperately, on to certain beliefs in spite of the fact that the evidence is all against the likelihood of these beliefs being true.

It is high time that we Christians shook off our reticence and shouted out loud and clear that the true fact of the situation is that there is a strong case for the truth of the Gospel and the various parts of it. In a very small way this book will try to show something of that case.

Doubt is not in itself a sinful thing. Doubt can be, and often is, a very healthy thing. Tennyson's famous words have still a lot to commend them: 'There is more faith in honest doubt, believe me, than in half the creeds'.

But belief beats unbelief; and belief has much more to support it. I believe in the Christian Faith.

I believe in the Christian Faith because I have seen it work in other people's experience; because I have found it to work in my own experience; because it is the best hope I know for a better society and a better world; and because it has a great volume of evidence to back up its claim to be true.

In support of my position I will now proceed to enumerate some of the elements of this Christian Faith to which I subscribe; and attempt to explain why I believe in them, and why there seems good reason for others to believe in them too.

1
I believe in the Bible

I BELIEVE in the Bible. I believe it is by far the most important book in the world. This is because it contains the most important news the world could ever hear, the story of God's dealings with mankind and, in particular, the message of the eternal life he has made available to mankind through Jesus Christ.

In the Bible we may discover what God is like and at the same time what he would wish men and women to be like. Here we find the story of how he came to earth in an amazing act of love, and of how in an extension of that act of love he gave himself up sacrificially to be crucified on the Cross of Calvary, in order that all who choose to do so might enter eternal life both in this world and the world to come.

In other words, I believe in the Bible because the Bible tells me about Jesus. To read the Bible is to learn more of Jesus and to learn more of him is at the same time to learn more of God. The better we know the Bible, the better we know God and the more fully, as a result, our lives may be enriched by him, and the more sure our eternal hope may become.

It is extremely important, therefore, that we should read the Bible with understanding: and it is wise to bear in mind certain things that could hinder or even impair that understanding, certain things that the Bible is not, but which it is sometimes thought to be.

(1) The Bible is *not* a book of magic handed down to us from heaven, full of guaranteed spells and incantations of

a spiritual kind. It is not intended to be used as if it were that kind of book. But sometimes, unfortunately, it is. I myself have known people who have treated it as if it were just such a repository of magical words, turning it up quite at random in the confident expectation that whatever of its words might hit their eyes would be a message sent to them direct from God. This is a serious misunderstanding and a gross misuse of the Bible.

To employ the Bible in this manner is not greatly dissimilar to the process some people adopt of shutting their eyes and then sticking a pin among a list of runners in a horse race in the hope that the pin-pointed name will be the name of the winner. There is really no more likelihood of a favourable outcome in the former instance than in the latter.

There is a very old, much told and no doubt apocryphal, tale of a man who treated the Bible in this very fashion. Finding himself in a situation of considerable difficulty, and feeling desperately in need of guidance, he decided to turn to the Bible for assistance. Holding it in his hand, he said to himself, 'I will let the Good Book fall open in my hand and, whatever words my eyes light upon first, I will take to be the Lord's words to me'.

He did just as he intended, and the first words he saw were, 'Judas went out and hanged himself'. This did not appear to be at all helpful, so he concluded that there must be some mistake and decided to try again. This time the words he caught were, 'Go and do thou likewise'. Not relishing this either as an answer to his problem, he chose to make a third attempt. This time the message received was, 'What thou hast to do, do quickly'.

I imagine—and certainly hope—that he thereupon abandoned that particular method of seeking scriptural guidance. This story illustrates how unwise and even dangerous it can be to follow such a course with regard to the Bible. The Bible is not a repository of facile, instant remedies for human ailments which may be obtained by the simple process of letting the Bible fall open any old how. The Bible, on the contrary, needs to be read with as much care and wisdom and understanding as we can muster.

(2) The Bible is *not* just one book. It is, in fact, a library of no less than 66 different books, written at different times by different authors, using different styles and even different languages.

The Bible, at the same time, may fittingly be referred to as *The* Book, for there is a strong thread of unity running through it that binds all its pages together. That thread of unity is its witness to God and to God's way.

I do not mean to suggest by this statement that the Bible's witness to God is uniform at every point, nor indeed that it is always one hundred per cent accurate.

The Bible is not itself the revelation of God, it is the *record* of God's revelation of himself, a revelation made through the events of history; through men and women of history such as the prophets; and supremely through Jesus. That is to say, God did not dictate the Bible. The Bible does not consist of the *words* of God. It is rather the record made by devoted and inspired men of God's endeavours to make himself clearly known to an often unwilling and unperceptive mankind, culminating in the perfect revelation of himself in Jesus. The Bible, although it is not to be identified with the words of God, certainly contains the *Word* of God.

The authors of the various books that make up the Bible, devoted and inspired as they were, were still human and therefore not infallible. The consequence was that at times they may have failed to understand fully or to understand altogether clearly what they were recording; and at times they may not have remembered with absolute accuracy.

This is more frequently the situation in the Old Testament which tells the story of mankind groping upwards after an ever clearer vision of God. The trouble was that while God was always more than willing to let himself be known, mankind was rarely altogether willing and ready to receive that knowledge.

When we come to the New Testament, we read how God was at last made fully known when 'The Word was made flesh' in Jesus. The New Testament records how the Christian Faith was founded, not on mere human speculation and deduction, but on actual historical events which are verifiable and sure.

(3) The Bible is *not*—or need not be—dull or boring. It is true that it contains some dull passages like the 'A begat B and B begat C' parts in the Authorized (or King James) Version of the earlier Old Testament books. But very little of it is really dull. Much of it is in fact quite thrilling and exciting.

I am forced to admit that some things have conspired to give the casual reader an impression of dullness. The sometimes old-fashioned language and idiom of the King James Version, which gave to nearly all of my generation their first acquaintance with the Bible, can be very off-putting. Beautiful literature though it is, it can at times obscure the sense and make the reading of it a bit tedious.

In addition, the old method of printing the King James Version in small, cramped print made it eye-straining and uncomfortable to read.

But when the Bible is read in a well set out, clear-type modern translation, it is found to be a library of books that is very easy and pleasant to read.

(4) I also believe this about the Bible. What is at least as important to bear in mind as anything said thus far, in relation to reading the Bible with maximum understanding and profit, is that the Bible is *not*—and does not claim to be—an authority on every conceivable subject under the sun. The Bible is, I believe, the most important book in the world; but it is a *religious* book. The intention is to tell us of God, and of God's dealings with mankind, and to help us find our way to God. In pursuing this most important religious purpose, the Bible frequently says some remarkably fine and illuminating things about other subjects. But God is its chosen subject and it is not to be taken as a text book of, say, science or geology.

In a kind of way, the Bible is a bit like the Highway Code. The Highway Code does not tell us anything about growing tomatoes or weather forecasting, but it is indispensable for its own subject, namely how to behave on the roads. In a similar fashion the Bible is not an authority on all subjects, but it is indispensable for the business of travelling properly on the road of life.

There is this, too. There is little chance of a man passing his driving test if he chooses to ignore the Highway Code and disregard its instructions and advice. Similarly, the man who disregards the Bible and what it has to say will have little chance of passing his ultimate test at the end of the day.

What is more, apart from the question of passing or failing his test, the motorist who drives in disobedience of the Highway Code inevitably brings pain and trouble and sorrow upon others, as well as upon him (or her) self. Just so, the person who insists on living his life in defiance of the Bible, its message and its teaching, will cause hurt to himself and to others, and can never know the best of life even in this world.

This is what I believe about the Bible: not that it is an

authority on all subjects, but that it is essential for the job in hand, that of living life well and of getting to our destination in the end. Psalm 119 says in verse 105 (Authorized Version), 'Thy word is a lamp unto my feet, and a light unto my path'. The picture represented is of a man travelling at night in a dark, uncertain terrain with a lantern to guide his way. Now, a lantern is not the sun, making everything clear, but it lights up the immediate area. It shows the traveller where to put his feet; it helps him to avoid the pitfalls; it enables him to find his way.

Just so, the Bible does not shed light on every subject, nor answer every question. But it provides ample illumination for anyone to know his duty and to find his way home to God.

2
I believe in the Gospels

THE CULMINATION of God's self-revelation was, and is, in Jesus. Because of that, the four little writings that are called the Gospels are the most important of all writings, since they contain the only written records the world possesses of the life, death and resurrection of the most important person ever born. I believe in these Gospels.

I believe that they are historically reliable. It is undoubtedly of tremendous importance that we should be able to have confidence that the Gospel records are so reliable; and I believe that there are very good grounds for just such confidence.

Those who believe that God actually dictated the Gospels (along with the rest of the Bible), or at least personally supervised every word that the various writers wrote, do not, of course, require any other ground other than this to be confident that the Gospels are true—although they may have other very considerable difficulties to face.

Most Christians, however, are like me, glad to be able to find other assurance that the Gospels are historically reliable. I believe there is a large volume of such assurance to be had and many good grounds for counting them trustworthy.

The chief source of confidence is simply the manner in which the Gospels came into being. The stages of their evolution are fenced all along the way with safeguards of reliability. If we take a look at these stages, I will try to explain what I mean.

There were three main stages in the process which eventually gave us these four little books which we call

7

the Gospels, three stages which were not rigidly exclusive but which were, nevertheless, quite distinct from each other.

First, there was the *Stage of Happening*, the actual taking place on earth, in the context of history, of the Jesus story. This was especially that period of about three years during which Jesus, as we sometimes put it, 'performed his ministry'. He left his home in Nazareth and became an itinerant preacher, moving through the length and breadth of Palestine, preaching about the nature and the will of God and doing many deeds of help and healing.

The *Stage of Happening* reached its climax when Jesus journeyed to Jerusalem for what turned out to be his final visit to that holy city. This visit culminated in his being arrested and put to trial. After his condemnation, execution and burial, he was raised from the dead—so his followers claimed—and appeared to them many times over a period of some six weeks before finally withdrawing his visible presence from them.

Next came the *Stage of Oral Tradition*, when the Jesus story was carried on and handed down *mainly* by word of mouth. I have laid stress on the word 'mainly' in this context because the perpetuation of the story of Jesus was never exclusively by speech alone. Even while he was still alive, some of his friends, it appears very likely, wrote down, perhaps in the form of diary notes, some reminiscences of Jesus and his words and deeds. Once the *Stage of Happening* was ended and the *Stage of Oral Tradition* was begun, there began also a steady increase in the volume of the writing down about Jesus.

There was nothing very systematic about it in the earlier years, and most of what was committed to writing was of a fragmentary nature. But there was a definite overlapping into the stage of speech by the *Stage of Writing* which was to follow.

None of the earlier writings has survived independently, although there is good reason to believe that some of them have been incorporated in whole or in part in one or more of the Gospels.

The Oral Tradition, the passing on of reminiscences of Jesus by word of mouth, was like a river flowing along two main channels—one in the missionary preaching of the Christians and the other in the worship of their assembling together on the Lord's Day. In both of these spheres the stories of Jesus continued to be told and re-told week after week.

Finally came the *Stage of Writing*. This stage in the evolutionary process which gave birth to the four Gospels arrived when the ranks of those who had personal knowledge of the *Stage of Happening* began to grow very thin. As time and persecution took increasing toll, the numbers of those who had known Jesus in the flesh became fewer and fewer. When this time came, the Christian Church felt more and more the need to have at least some of the more important parts of the story of Jesus committed to writing.

The Gospels of Mark, of Matthew, of Luke and of John were written in response to that felt need to preserve the reminiscences concerning Jesus in a more definite and more permanent form. When this stage arrived, those who took on the task of compiling the written records found a mass of material ready to hand. Each of the four evangelists took this material, both oral and written, examined it, assessed and sifted it, then they made selections from it and presented to the Church—and so to the world—the four short books which stand now at the beginning of the New Testament.

Some will find sufficient substantiation of the historical reliability of the Gospels simply in remembering how the testimonies of original eye-witnesses were passed on down the years until finally a selection of their content was enshrined in the written Gospels. That evolutionary process itself is an indication that these Gospels have come to us as substantially accurate transcriptions of the original stories.

In addition, however, we are able to cite a number of factors which ensure the accuracy of the oral transmission of the Jesus story.

(1) There is, for one, the *continuity* of the transmission. It was handed down in a continuity that was unbroken. There *never* was a time when the stories of Jesus were not being repeated among the Christians and by the Christians; *never* a time when the Church lacked the historical tradition of Jesus. The continuous nature of the transmission must have made it extremely difficult, if not impossible, for any serious error to creep in.

Supposing a Church of the present day was some 35 years old and had continuously, from its very beginning, made a point of reciting with regular frequency a narrative of the events which had brought it into being. Could there be any reasonable doubt that the narrative was still substantially the same as it had been originally? Similarly, must not the tradition of Jesus, having been continuously perpetuated by the Church, have come down to the time of the Gospels substantially as it had been first reported?

(2) Side by side with that may be placed the phenomenal *power of memory* possessed by the Jews of that time. It was far superior to anything that Westerners are accustomed to; and the accuracy of their verbal transmissions was by any standards quite remarkable. Beginning with a natural aptitude for memory-work little paralleled in the Western world, they had enhanced this skill by choosing

to do most of their teaching and learning by word of mouth—books, in any event, before the invention of printing, were a comparatively rare commodity. The result was the development of memories of remarkable accuracy.

(3) There was the *public nature* of the oral transmission. The preservation and the passing on of the stories of Jesus in this 'oral period' was never the concern of only a hand-picked minority among the Christians. It was never the case that the oral tradition was the property and the care of a limited number who handed it down privately from one to the other until the time came when that tradition was made public through the Gospels. From the outset the tradition was the property of the whole Church, and the Church as a whole acted as its guardian. There is little doubt, therefore, that if ever any major deviation from the original had been attempted—whether by accident or design—a whole chorus of voices would have been raised at once in protest, and correction demanded and obtained.

(4) There was the presence of *eye-witnesses.* We can not reasonably imagine, as sometimes we appear to do, that as soon as the first proclamation of the Jesus story was made, every eye-witness withdrew completely and forever from the scene. The fact is that, right up to and including the time the tradition was set down in writing, surviving eye-witnesses of the original events were on hand to check the accuracy of its transmissions. Their oversight of the tradition in transmission must have been more than sufficient to ensure its substantial trustworthiness.

No serious deviation from the original event could possibly have occurred with them on the scene.

(5) There was the presence of a *knowledgeable oppo-sition*. In the oral period, the stories of Jesus were being rehearsed frequently in the hearing of unbelievers—many of them hostile—as well as of believers. This must have helped in no small measure to ensure that these stories suffered no substantial change in the course of their repetition. The uncommitted, and particularly the hostile uncommitted, would have been only too quick to seize on any feature of the Christians' story which did not tally with its previous telling, and to exploit that discrepancy to the full.

The result was that, both in their public preaching and also in debate and discussion, it would be out of the question for the Christians to vary their story in any material aspect from one telling to another.

The opposition confronting the proclamation of the Gospel message in those early years was a formidable thing. To a great many people the new Christian sect was hateful and harmful; and they were most anxious to have it destroyed. Among them were some of the most able men of the day, highly intelligent, learned, and skilled in the art of debate. If the Christians had been guilty of inconsistencies in the repetition of their reminiscences of Jesus, if they had been found to be making any substantial changes in their story as they continued to repeat it, they would quickly have been exposed to ridicule and contempt and their preaching would have been routed from the field.

(6) There was also the circumstance that the preaching of the first Christians, which began simultaneously with the Church itself, was primarily concerned with the *historical facts of Jesus*. Sometimes we seem to have the idea that the history of Jesus and the message of the early Church were quite separate things. On the contrary, however, the

history and the message were largely one and the same thing.

In the first recorded sermon of the Christian Church, the apostle Peter said, among other things, '. . . this Jesus, delivered up according to the definite plan and foreknowledge of God, you crucified and killed by the hands of lawless men. But God raised him up having loosed the pangs of death, because it was not possible for him to be held by it' (Acts 2:22-24, Revised Standard Version). Those words indicate the burden of the preaching of the early Church and indicate at the same time how paramount from the beginning was the interest in the historical Jesus.

This is further borne out by the statement made by Peter when he was advising the disciple band to appoint someone to their number as a replacement for the lapsed Judas: 'So one of the men who have accompanied us during all the time that the Lord Jesus went in and out among us . . . one of these men must become with us a witness to his resurrection' (Acts 1:21-22, Revised Standard Version). This statement makes it clear that the primary task of a disciple was to communicate the story of Jesus, particularly of his resurrection, and that the chief qualification for discipleship was intimate personal knowledge of the historical events of Jesus's life.

All this makes it plain, in turn, that for the early Church nothing mattered so much as the historical facts concerning Jesus. Apart from these, there was simply no Gospel, no message worth passing on; and the accurate proclamation of these facts was, therefore, not only the chief content of the Church's preaching, but also the Church's chief concern.

I would like now to draw attention to some features of the Gospels and their evolution which strengthen my confidence in their historical reliability, even though some of them may seem at first sight to be a threat to that confidence.

(a) There is what may appear to the Western world of the twentieth century a disturbingly long gap between the *Stage of Happening* and the *Stage of Writing*. Some 30 years or more elapsed between the end of the happening stage and the appearance of the first of the Gospels (which was probably Mark). In our age, when anything counted noteworthy tends to get rushed into print immediately, that may seem a surprisingly long time, perhaps dangerously long.

There were, however, very good reasons for this lapse of time. Books were scarce and expensive to produce; and, since the first Christians expected the end of the world to come soon, the writing of books about Jesus seemed to them largely irrelevant and unnecessary. All the more so since, unlike us today, they placed a much higher value on the spoken word than on the written, particularly if the speaker was one who had unquestionable authority to speak.

So long, therefore, as there survived eye-witnesses with personal knowledge of Jesus and his story, there was little place and little welcome for the more impersonal written record. There was, in fact, no need for it until the ranks of the eye-witnesses became so thinned out as to create the real possibility of a time coming soon when there would be no one on hand in the Church to check from personal knowledge that the repetition of the Jesus story continued to be faithful to the historical facts.

It was in response to this felt need, and in order to guard against the risk of corruption, that the Gospels came to be written. This carries the corollary that the Christian Church was satisfied that the tradition had been transmitted with accuracy up to this point.

(b) The Gospels contain a number of 'difficult' sayings and allusions whose presence must have caused some perplexity or criticism and must have been an embarrassment to the Church. Their presence in the records can not be satisfactorily accounted for except on the basis of the Gospels being reliable representations of a reliable tradition.

I am thinking, for instance, of rather uncomplimentary references to the apostles. For example, in Matthew 16:23, Jesus says to Peter, 'Get behind me, Satan! You are a hindrance to me' (RSV): or in Mark 6:51-52, 'they had not understood the lesson of the loaves; their minds were dull' (Moffatt). Taking into account the high regard in which the whole Church held the apostles at the time the Gospels were written, the conclusion is inescapable that these Gospels must have been written with the utmost respect for accuracy. If not, such uncomplimentary references as these would never have been allowed to find a place in what were, after all, more or less official records. If the tradition had undergone any substantial alteration in the process of transmission, such 'inconvenient' items would surely have been among the first to be eliminated or at least drastically revised.

(c) The Gospel records do not agree with one another at every point; at times they are in marked contrast and even, apparently, in contradiction. At first it might appear very disturbing and cast doubt on their essential trustworthiness that such differences should exist, but in fact the reverse is true. Their presence is totally consistent with what we should expect to find in separate and reliable accounts.

Suppose some dramatic event has taken place—a street accident, say—and you ask a few eye-witnesses to write down their version of what happened, you will almost certainly get some startling variations between the individual accounts. But if your eye-witnesses are honest and reliable, you will find them agreeing on the main points of the story. This is exactly the kind of situation that the Gospels reflect.

If the Gospel narratives had corresponded exactly on each and every point, we would have been compelled to view them with some suspicion and to wonder if there had been some measure of collusion and 'a cooking of the books'. But the mixture they present of agreement on major points and disagreement on some lesser points is just what is to be expected in records that enshrine a tradition originally derived from eye-witnesses and faithfully handed down.

I believe in the Gospels as being documents substantially faithful to the historical events they record. I hold to this belief because I am convinced that a number of factors have combined to ensure that faithfulness, not least the process by which they evolved into the finished products which stand now at the beginning of our New Testament.

I am reminded of a party game we sometimes used to play when I was young. The company spaced itself out in a circle round the room and then the one delegated for the task whispered a message into the ear of one of the circle. He in turn whispered the message, or what he had understood it to be, into the ear of the next in line—and so on round the circle until it came back to the one who had started it off. The object of the exercise was to see how accurately the message would survive in transmission —or, rather, to see how inaccurately it might reach its goal. Some very hilarious corruptions were liable to arise —reminiscent at times of the apocryphal tale of the message passed from the front line to the rear during the first World War. It began, as 'Send reinforcements; we are going to advance' and reached its destination as 'Send three and fourpence; we are going to a dance'.

I quote this party game not because it resembles the manner in which the four Gospels came into being, but, rather, because the process of evolution of the Gospels had so many important differences *from* it.

Imagine that the room in which the game is played is one in which people are continually coming and going. To begin the proceedings, some of the company narrate to the others events which they and some companions, also present in the room at the moment, had witnessed only that afternoon.

From then on that very story is told and re-told continuously—both by the original narrators and by others—while all the time there are departures and new arrivals. This more closely resembles the circumstances under which the oral tradition was transmitted.

Imagine now that there are several rooms, not merely one, with free passage between them; and imagine that the same story is told in each, but by different eyewitnesses. Imagine too, that as the evening wears on, more and more people begin to write down parts of the story. Imagine, finally, that at the end of the evening, four people who, if not present from the start, have at least been present for a considerable time, write down a systematic version of the story, with other knowledgeable people assisting them to keep it faithful to the original version.

This picture gives a rough representation of the process of evolution which took the Jesus tradition from the *Stage of Happening* through the *Stage of Speech* into the *Stage of Writing* and the production of the Gospels. I am convinced that the process allowed little room for any substantial deviation from the actual historical events they purport to record, to intrude into these Gospels; and so I believe firmly in their trustworthiness.

3
I believe in the Resurrection of Jesus

I BELIEVE that Jesus was raised from the dead. The Resurrection of Jesus is the foundation point of the Christian Gospel; the *sine qua non*. As a former Archbishop of Canterbury, A M Ramsey, once said: 'For the first disciples the Gospel without the Resurrection was not merely a Gospel without its final chapter: it was not a Gospel at all' (*The Resurrection of Christ*, A M Ramsey, Fontana, 1945, p 9). The Apostle Paul makes an identical affirmation in 1 Corinthians 15:14: 'If Christ was not raised, then our Gospel is null and void, and so is your faith' (RSV).

The Resurrection of Jesus is the centrepiece of the Gospel and the heart of the message; I believe it to be historically true. I believe it to be a fact of history that Jesus of Nazareth who was crucified to death, was raised to life again after his crucifixion, and that he continues to live now.

It is little wonder, all the same, that many people have found difficulty in accepting the Resurrection as true. It was and is a most extraordinary event, surely the most extraordinary of all time. Many people have adopted the position that any alternative explanation of the facts is preferable to admitting that a dead man may have been miraculously restored to life. Someone once said, 'If the evidence were fifty times stronger than it is, I still would not believe'.

That dismissive attitude is not only common, it is also perfectly understandable—the Resurrection of Jesus from the dead does take a lot of believing. This attitude is nevertheless—dare I say it?—the very same kind of unscientific attitude which Christians are often, and sometimes justifiably, accused of adopting; namely that of making up one's mind without proper reference to the evidence, or even making it up *in spite of* the evidence.

The truly scientific attitude would be not to rule out the possibility of the Resurrection as being *ipso facto* something that simply could not have happened. The truly scientific attitude will come to the relevant evidence with an open mind and let the evidence determine what conclusion is to be drawn.

I believe that the evidence in favour of the historical truth of the Resurrection of Jesus is tremendously strong, so strong as to be overwhelming and, from any reasonable standpoint, irresistible.

An indication of the strength of that case will, I hope, be given by the following relevant factors:

(1) There is, to begin with, the evidence of the New Testament. This evidence is two-fold. There is the simple fact that the New Testament exists; and there is the fact that the whole of the New Testament affirms that Jesus was raised from the dead after his crucifixion.

It is an obvious fact that the New Testament exists, as indeed it has done now for many centuries; and it is extremely difficult even to offer a plausible explanation of how it came into being, unless we accept that the event at its heart—the Resurrection of Jesus—actually took place. Without that event the emergence of the New Testament becomes an extraordinary phenomenon that is impossible to account for in any satisfactory manner.

It is also a clear fact that the New Testament bears unanimous witness to the Resurrection of Jesus. According to A M Hunter, 'The whole New Testament literature is radiant with the light of the Resurrection' (*Life and Words of Jesus,* A M Hunter, p 123).

Such testimony cannot easily be dismissed. Should it not, therefore, be counted decisive unless some satisfactory counter-explanation is offered; and a really convincing alternative explanation of it is not easy to find. By far the most persuasive explanation of the New Testament's witness to the Resurrection of Jesus is that it really did happen.

While all of the New Testament makes its witness to the Resurrection, six of its writers more explicitly affirm that fact. The four evangelists, along with Paul and Peter, each declare that Jesus, crucified to death on a Roman cross, was raised to life again. In their different ways, all give their independent corroboration, and this adds up to testimony that cannot lightly be disregarded. In most courts of enquiry the fact that six independent witnesses corroborated each other that a certain incident had taken place would be taken as conclusive evidence that it had.

Some may query my use of the word 'independent' in connection with the Resurrection testimony of these six New Testament writers. For it is well known that, in the writing of their Gospels, both Matthew and Luke made borrowings from the earlier Mark, at times quoting him quite extensively. This, however, does not seem to me to detract from the independence of their witness to the fact of the Resurrection. They were all willing to append their signature to an affidavit that Jesus of Nazareth had been raised from the dead.

The important thing is that all six of these writers were in a position to have a good knowledge of the real facts of the case, either as eye-witnesses or by using information derived ultimately from those who were. Whatever their differences in situation or in background, they all agree in their declaration that Jesus had been raised from the dead.

To be sure, they do not say so in exactly the same

way. More than that, it must be admitted that there are disagreements between their various accounts of the Resurrection event and sometimes these disagreements amount to contradictions that are difficult to reconcile. At the same time, there would be much more concern for the apologist if there were no such differences at all. If the accounts had harmonised in every detail, it would have been difficult to avoid the suspicion that perfect harmonisation had been artificially contrived in order not to 'rock the boat'.

Despite the serious problems raised by some of the contradictions, what we hear in the Resurrection testimony of these six writers is, broadly speaking, the very thing we should expect to find, given that the writers were honest men and that the event they were alluding to was the most surprising and the most exciting the world had ever witnessed.

Suppose two cars collide in a busy street of a busy town; and suppose you seize hold of six witnesses of the event and ask each of them to write down his or her version of the incident. Almost certainly their accounts will contain marked differences. At the same time, if they are honestly trying to give accurate reports, they will agree on the main features of the event. They will be sure, at least, to agree that the accident took place in that town on that day.

This illustration is somewhat like the witness of these six New Testament writers concerning the Resurrection of Jesus. There are differences between their various versions—startling differences at times—but they are unanimous on the main points and more emphatically on the central fact that Jesus was raised to life after his death on the cross. On the whole their differences add up to, rather than detract from, their general ring of authenticity. What after all are their differences compared with their tremendous agreement?

(2) There is the evidence of the existence of the Christian Church. Like the New Testament, the Church is an undeniable fact, and its existence cannot reasonably be explained unless the belief in the Resurrection of Jesus, which brought it into existence, is also based on fact.

That it was the belief in the Resurrection which brought the Church into being is, I think, a premise that is universally accepted. At least, so far as I know, no one has ever disputed it. Without his followers' belief in his Resurrection, Jesus would never have been heard of beyond his immediate circle, or beyond his own time. The very existence of the Christian Church is extremely difficult to account for, unless that belief was founded on historical fact.

Any theory of delusion or fraud is something that requires a much greater stretching of the imagination than even the resurrection to life of an executed felon.

(3) There is the closely-allied fact that the Church and the public proclamation of the Resurrection both originated in Jerusalem, and did so hard on the heels of the alleged events. Had it all been the result of a delusion or a trick? Is there any likelihood—any possibility even—that the preposterous claim that Jesus had been raised from the dead could have survived at that time and in that place?

Consider the situation. About seven weeks after Jesus had been executed by crucifixion in Jerusalem and buried there, some of his erstwhile friends and followers began to declare publicly in the streets of that same city that he had been raised from the dead and was alive again. If their claim was false—whether or not they themselves believed it to be true—would it have had any chance of survival there, particularly so soon after the alleged event?

If the Resurrection of Jesus did not actually happen, those who were asserting that it had could scarcely have chosen a worse place to begin their preaching. If the Resurrection claim was untrue it would have been so easy to disprove it there and then. All that would have been needed, for instance, was to point out the tomb where the body of Jesus was mouldering away—and there were plenty of people on hand who would have wasted no time in doing just that, if they could. Jerusalem was a small city and that would have been no problem.

There were many in Jerusalem bitterly hostile to the new Christian faith and to the Resurrection claim on which it was founded. A considerable number of these were men of influence and authority. With such opposition to contend with, it is inconceivable that the preaching of the Resurrection could have survived for any length of time, far less made the progress it did, unless it were based on solid historical truth.

Look at it another way. It is as though there were two teams of gladiators in conflict in the city of Jerusalem shortly after the crucifixion of Jesus. On the one hand there was the little band of Jesus people claiming that he was risen from the dead. This group consisted for the most part of men and women of little wealth or position, who were unskilled in the arts of rhetoric and debate. On the other hand there were the leaders and administrators of the well-organised religious system that centred on the Temple in Jerusalem: the high-priest and his associates and followers. These were men of much wealth and power. In addition, a number of them were well versed in debating skills, and some were actually lawyers.

Jesus had a lot of enemies in Jerusalem. They had brought about his death. Naturally they fervently desired to keep him dead. It would appear that all the odds were in their favour in the 'gladiatorial' clash in Jerusalem some 2000 years ago; and it is almost incredible that they should lose the contest. And yet we know that they did.

Can we find any reasonable explanation for their defeat except that the Resurrection claim they were opposing was really true?

(4) There is the fact of the astonishing change that took place in Jesus's disciples over that first Easter weekend. It was a transformation so remarkable that only the fact of the Resurrection of Jesus can satisfactorily explain it.

On the evening of Good Friday they were crushed and broken. Their Master, whom they had loved so dearly, and from whom they had expected so much, was dead. Even worse, he had been done to death on a Roman cross and the Scriptures seemed to indicate that such a death meant God's disfavour had rested on him. Not only had they lost him forever, but clearly he had not been the Messiah after all. Surely God would never have permitted such an ignominious ending to his life if he had been.

No wonder they were disillusioned and in despair. No wonder they were skulking behind closed doors, fearful of being arrested by the authorities and perhaps being made to share in their leader's fate. No wonder they were waiting only for the Sabbath to be over, and its travelling restrictions ended, so that they could escape from the city and get back to Galilee where they might lick their wounds and forget the disappointment of it all.

Over that weekend something occurred that totally changed them. Their gloom became gladness, their despair gave way to hope, their fear was replaced by courage. Before very long they were back out on the streets of that very same city where they had been recently intent only on saving their own skins, boldly proclaiming the name of Jesus regardless of the risks involved to themselves.

It needs something very drastic to explain the transformation which was effected in the disciples over that historic weekend. They said it was the discovery that Jesus was risen. It is exceedingly difficult to find any other explanation that will meet the case.

(5) There is the fact of the empty tomb. It is a fact that brooks no real argument that the grave in which Jesus was placed after his crucifixion was found to be empty of his body on Easter morning.

It may well be sufficient simply to point out that from the outset the emptiness of the tomb was accepted by friend and foe alike. When the Resurrection preaching began, the opposition did not bring it to an abrupt halt by pointing to Jesus's grave and his body lying in it. If they have been able to do that, they surely would have done it. Instead, they offered an alternative explanation of the tomb's vacancy—'His disciples stole the body' (Matthew 28:13, New English Bible). They did not attempt to dispute that the grave was no longer occupied.

If, then, the tomb of Jesus was empty on Easter Day, that fact is best explained by accepting the claim of his friends that he had been raised from the dead. Extraordinary though this claim might seem, it is the one that most satisfactorily meets the requirements of the situation. No other explanation will do.

The accusation by the opposition, that the disciples had stolen the body, does not stand up to scrutiny. Note the following points:

(a) It is difficult to imagine that the building of the Christian Church could have been founded on a deliberate falsehood. The fact that its founder had taught an ethic of uncompromising honesty makes it extremely improbable that his followers could have, or would have, pursued any such course.

(b) It is difficult to imagine that a known deception like this could have inspired in the first followers of Jesus such enthusiasm as they showed for it and such willing-ness to endure sacrifice and even martyrdom on its behalf.

(c) It is difficult to imagine that there was anyone in the band of disciples capable of planning and executing such a deception successfully, in view of the quite enor-mous practical difficulties to be overcome before an abduction of the body could be accomplished without detection.

(d) It is difficult to imagine, since the origins of the Christian Church would have been based on what am-ounted to a successful fraud, that not one of those who were part of the deception would have given the game away, particularly in view of the sufferings and per-secutions that ensued.

It is, therefore, an extremely improbable proposition that the friends of Jesus secretly removed his body from the tomb sometime between the Friday evening and first light on the Sunday morning.

Any suggestion that the body was removed by the enemies of Jesus has nothing to commend it either. There can be no doubt that if this had been the case, just as soon as the Resurrection claim was voiced, some enemies of Jesus would have announced loudly and clearly the true explanation of the empty tomb. It would have demolish-ed that Resurrection claim very effectively if they had made it public that, 'The grave is empty because we moved the body. We can show you where it now lies rotting away'. The fact that they made no such protest can be explained only by assuming that they were unable to substantiate it.

It has at times been suggested as another alternative that perhaps Jesus was not really dead when taken down from the cross and buried. Although having all the appear-ance of death, he revived in the tomb, made his escape and rejoined his disciples to induce in them the belief that he had risen from the dead.

This suggestion, famous in its time and often referred to as the 'Swoon Theory', was first put forward in the middle of the nineteenth century. It has long since been discredited. Nevertheless, it keeps reappearing in some form or other and for this reason alone deserves to be looked at here. It is a theory which may be seen to fly in the face of many facts and probabilities:

(a) Its necessary basic assumption that Jesus was not really dead is a highly unlikely one. It was the task of the Roman execution squad to put their prisoners to death and to ensure that the execution was properly carried out. It is quite incredible that any prisoner they pronounced dead could still have even a spark of life left in him.

(b) If, however, for argument's sake, it is supposed that this Jesus was indeed only in some kind of comatose condition when laid in his tomb, the difficulties facing the Swoon Theory are still immense. It asks us to believe that Jesus, more dead than alive, physically very weak after the 'scourging' and the crucifixion, not only regained consciousness after the burial, but was somehow able to struggle free from the grave clothes that bound him. And that somehow also, although working from inside the tomb where very little purchase against the stone that blocked the entrance could be obtained, he was able to move aside that massive rolling stone and so make good his escape. Is it credible?

(c) If, again for the sake of argument, we take this theory a stage further, it now asks us to believe that this Jesus, having escaped from the tomb, but obviously weak and naked, somehow made his way undetected to rejoin his disciples. More than that, it asks us to believe that this bedraggled and naked figure convinced the disciples not that he had survived crucifixion, but that he had risen from the dead. Despite his physical condition, which must have required a lot of care and attention, despite the fact that he must later have died and stayed dead, the Swoon Theory asks us to believe that Jesus convinced his disciples that he had *conquered* death, for that belief was undoubtedly the basis of their preaching and the foundation of the Church. Is it credible that such an escape from the tomb could have produced such a belief?

(6) To continue with more evidence in favour of the truth of the Resurrection, let us examine the fact that Jesus, after his death and burial, was seen and spoken with by a considerable number of people. No one would deny that these 'appearances' of the Risen Jesus were believed in wholeheartedly by the disciples, but it has been suggested that they may have been mistaken, and that far from being real these 'appearances' were some kind of hallucination.

I would argue that the appearances of Jesus after his crucifixion do not meet the requirements of hallucination. First, it is evident that the disciples were not expecting the Resurrection. Hallucinations come about through the impact of an expectation upon the subconscious. The disciples, however, far from expecting to see Jesus again, found considerable difficulty in accepting the fact of the Resurrection even after it occurred. Second, the disciples were scarcely the right type to be the subjects of hallucinations. For the most part hard-headed and materialistic, they were not likely to be ensnared by flights of fancy. And third, the appearances of the Risen Jesus were of a different character from that which hallucinations normally possess. They were not, as is usual, momentary, but were often prolonged interviews. They did not, as is usual, proceed with mounting frequency for a time and then tail gradually away; they took place over a limited period and then ceased abruptly and completely. And they did not, as is usual, leave their subjects exhausted; instead they left them invigorated.

(7) There is the fact that many who began by being passionately hostile and fiercely sceptical, came to accept the truth of the Resurrection and to embrace the new faith which that event had sparked off.

In the very earliest days members of the priestly faction were among the converts. They must have been about the most unlikely people in all history to be persuaded that the Resurrection of Jesus was historically true—unless it was. After all, they and their colleagues had been instrumental in bringing about the death of Jesus and they were delighted that they had managed to do so. They were also on the spot of the alleged event both in time and in place. No one was ever in a better position than they were to confirm that the Resurrection claim was false, if indeed it was.

A few years later one of the most eminent intellects of all time was won over to the new faith. Saul of Tarsus, who previously had hated, ridiculed and attacked the Resurrection claim, became firmly convinced that it was true. Saul was on the 'inside', had access to all the available evidence, was acquainted with all the arguments against the fact of the Resurrection and, in addition, was a man of outstanding learning and intelligence. He was certainly not one to be easily taken in by a trick or a deception of a Resurrection story. Add to this his intense prejudice against what seemed to him initially a blasphemous claim, then it is clear that he could and would have been persuaded to change from disbelief to belief only if the evidence for the Resurrection was, despite himself, recognised as irrefutable and irresistible.

It seems to me therefore that only if the Resurrection of Jesus is historically true can these seven facts above find a satisfactory explanation. The evidence is overwhelming. And so I believe that Jesus was raised from the dead at the first Easter.

4

I believe in the Incarnation

I BELIEVE in the uniqueness of Jesus. I believe that he was—and is—the Son of God. I believe that we are all God's sons and daughters; but I believe that Jesus was and is God's son in a very special sense.

The Christian Church has been accustomed from early times to speak of Jesus as the Son of God. He was so different, so special, that they found it impossible to describe him solely in human terms, and so they called him the Son of God.

Another way employed to define the uniqueness of Jesus has been to speak of him as divine. Again it would be in line with orthodox Christian thinking to say that there is something of divinity in all of us. But Jesus, it is claimed, was God Incarnate. God became man in Jesus; in Jesus the Word was made flesh. That is the Christian belief and I subscribe to it. Jesus was so remarkable that only such terms can even begin to define him.

I believe in the Incarnation. This means that I believe that Christmas is more than just a beautiful story—much more. It is not merely about any baby's birth. It is about the birth of a special baby, an unique child, truly human but at the same time more than human.

My belief that in Jesus, God became man is founded on the kind of person the baby Jesus came to be, the kind of things he said, the kind of things he did, the kind of life he lived, the kind of death he had and the kind of events that followed his death.

I believe in the Incarnation because it seems to me that the facts of Jesus's life cannot be explained with any

30

real satisfaction on any other basis. Jesus simply will not fit into any category that does not transcend the bounds of mere humanity. I for one, therefore, am compelled to believe with utter conviction that Jesus was much more than a very extraordinary man. I believe that there has been no other like him and that his uniqueness can be properly accounted for only by acknowledging that in him God took on human form.

As Peter, at Caesarea Philippi, once declared dramatically that Jesus was the Son of the living God, so must I. It was a quite staggering confession of faith that Peter made up there in the northern reaches of Galilee in the very shadow of Mount Hermon, for he was asserting that Jesus was unique not only in terms of his talents and his personality, but also in his relationship to God. He was saying, 'Jesus, you are supreme. You are God's Son in a way that no one else has been or can be'.

I also believe that whilst there is divinity in every human being, Jesus was uniquely divine. It was not a case however of God masquerading as a man; nor was Jesus some kind of hybrid creature who was half man and half God. Jesus, I believe, was fully human and fully divine at one and the same time.

I am in no doubt that he was fully human. and not simply acting out the part of a man. He really did, for example, experience heat and cold. When he walked through the fields and along the lanes of Galilee, he really felt the warmth of the sun on his back, and the breeze ruffling his hair. When he walked fast, he was compelled to breathe deeply; when he climbed a hill on a hot day, he perspired.

Jesus was truly human in terms of sharing the physical sensations that are common to all humanity. He was truly human also in terms of having to contend with the same kind of problems, trials and temptations, sorrows, joys and crises that are the universal lot of humankind.

When his father Joseph died, Jesus felt the sorrow of it just like the rest of the family, and along with them he wept for grief.

When, as the eldest son, he took over the family joinery business, he came to know, like other small businessmen in every age, the frustrations as well as the satisfactions of dealing with customers face to face. He knew what it was to undergo the stress of unreasonable demands and unfair criticism. He knew the temptation to be cross and irritable when things refused to go right, and the impulse to trade hot words back for hot words spoken.

When his hammer went astray and hit his thumb instead of a nail, it was real pain that Jesus felt. When he was crucified, the agony that he experienced was every bit as severe as the pain suffered by those hanging on the crosses erected on either side of him.

Indeed the humanity of Jesus was no charade. I once heard a man say, 'I believe that the baby Jesus lying in the manger already knew everything that was going to happen to him'. That is not my belief. It is not, as I see it, the picture of Jesus that the Gospels paint. It seems to make nonsense of his undoubted humanity, making him out to be no more than playing a part disguised as a man.

The truth is that, far from knowing as soon as he was born everything that was to befall him, Jesus saw his way emerge only gradually before him. This means, for instance, that his agony in Gethsemane was no counterfeit thing. It was, on the contrary, a very real agonising over the ultimate decision and a final bracing of himself to meet the terrible cost of following it through to its awful outcome.

It means, too, that the physical pain of his crucifixion was in no way diminished by the fact that he was 'the Word made flesh'.

I believe that Jesus was both fully human and fully divine. If I am asked to explain in any depth what exactly that means, I am forced to confess that the task is beyond me. I cannot properly understand it, far less explain it; but I am convinced that it is so. I believe in the Incarnation; I believe that in Jesus, God became man.

My belief in the Incarnation does not stand or fall on the truth of the Virgin Birth. To my mind the one is independent of the other. From early on, the Christian Church adopted as one of its tenets of belief that Jesus was born of a virgin mother. This still continues as an article of orthodox faith. But not all Christians are convinced that it was in this manner that Jesus made his entry into human life and experience. The evidence, they feel, is much less strong than for many other traditional Christian doctrines. More importantly, they maintain—and I agree with them—that what really matters is not the manner of Jesus's birth, but the fact of it.

Belief in the Incarnation is indeed identified in many minds with belief in the Virgin Birth; but they are not the same thing. The reality of the Incarnation does not depend on the historical truth of the Virgin Birth.

Many people, as a matter of fact, believe that the nature of God is such as to make it more likely that he would introduce his Saviour Son into the human experience through the normal process of procreation. The relevant evidence does not compel them to think otherwise.

Differences of opinion among Christians as to whether or not Jesus was born of a virgin are real and sincere. Neither view need, or should, be thought to cast suspicion on the genuine nature of the Christian faith of the person who subscribes to it. Nor ought it to be regarded as denying or diminishing the doctrine of the Incarnation.

I, for my part, am of the firm belief that the doctrine is

true. That is to say, I believe that in Jesus—however he
was born—God became man. 'The Word was made flesh
and dwelt among us' is the vivid and memorable way
that John's Gospel describes the event.

However exactly he came into the world, that baby
born in Bethlehem on the first Christmas Day has made
an enormous difference to the world and to countless
millions of men and women who have lived in it. That is
itself a mark of his uniqueness and an indication of his
deity.

How was he born who came to earth
With the God-light in his eyes?
Wrangle and argue about his birth
And yet you will not be wise.

And what does it matter? The clover blows
And the rose blooms on the tree,
And only God in heaven knows
How these things came to be.

You join in a thousand mysteries
That your wisdom can't explain
The green of the grass and the rolling seas
And the gold of the harvest grain.

And why do you bother your head . . . ?
And why does your faith grow dim?
You take the flower on the garden wall,
So why do you not take him?

5

I believe in the Crucifixion of Jesus

WHEN I DECLARE that I believe in the Crucifixion of Jesus, it means, to begin with, that I believe in it as a historical event. I believe it to be the case that on a certain day in Palestine, during the procuratorship of Pontius Pilate, Jesus of Nazareth was executed by crucifixion just outside the city wall of Jerusalem.

That execution was the culmination of some determined plotting and planning on the part of the religious leaders of the time. Because of this they managed in the end to force the procurator, rather against his will, to pass sentence of death on Jesus, authorisation of capital punishment being the perogative of the procurator alone.

It was a real crucifixion that Jesus underwent, not pretence. And crucifixion was a very cruel and very horrible thing.

In those days it was common for a man condemned to be crucified to be scourged, that is whipped, first of all; and Jesus likewise was scourged. Usually a condemned person was scourged after sentence had been passed, but in the case of Jesus it seems that Pilate had him scourged earlier in the proceedings in the vain hope that his enemies might be satisfied with that. The result, however, was just as painful, for scourging was an experience so agonising as to defy description.

It was carried out with an instrument called the *flagellum* (hence the alternative word 'flagellation'). The *flagellum* (or lash) was a long, leather whip which was usually studded with sharp objects such as pieces of rough metal and broken bone.

The prisoner was tied to a pillar so that he was unable to move and then this fiendish instrument was used to whip him across his bare back. The scourge inevitably took flesh from the victim's back every time it struck. Many men went mad under a scourging. Many died.

After the scourging, Jesus was marched, again following custom, to the place of execution, carrying the horizontal part of his cross as he went. He had, however, been so weakened physically by what he had gone through the preceding night and morning, particularly by the scourging, that he kept falling beneath the weight of the cross. The officer in charge of the execution conscripted Simon of Cyrene out of the crowd to carry it the rest of the way.

The actual process of crucifixion could take any one of several forms and all of them were extremely agonising—hence our word 'excruciating' to indicate very severe pain. Sometimes, when the condemned man reached the place of execution, the cross was placed in the socket already prepared in the ground. When it stood upright in position, the prisoner was lifted up and affixed to it.

Sometimes, the cross was laid flat upon the ground, the prisoner was pinned to it in that position, and then the cross was lifted upright and lowered heavily into its socket.

Sometimes the hands of the condemned man were tied to the cross with his arms outstretched; more often the hands were *nailed* to the wood.

Sometimes the feet were tied to the vertical beam of the cross; sometimes the feet were crossed and a single nail driven through them into the wood.

In the case of Jesus, while art and tradition have often tended to represent him as having nails driven through both hands and feet, it seems more likely that his hands were nailed and his feet bound. John's Gospel at any rate, in describing the appearance of the Risen Jesus to Thomas, speaks of the nail prints in the hands but makes no reference to nail prints in the feet.

In either event, Jesus must have suffered the most intense physical agony by the mere fact of being pinned to the cross.

Crucifixion must be one of the most cruel agencies of death that mankind has ever devised. When Jesus was affixed to his cross he was already in great pain from the earlier flagellation and the effects of the nails driven through his flesh. Now he was left to hang on that cross as the heat of the day grew in its intensity, his body forced into an unnatural and uncomfortable position, his increasing thirst steadily accentuating an agony from which there was never any possibility of respite or relief.

I believe in the crucifixion as an event of history. I believe in it also as an event of cosmic significance. I believe that when Jesus died on Calvary, something was achieved that affects the eternal destiny of all the human race. This achievement, whatever precisely it may have been, has for long been spoken of by students of the New Testament as the 'Atonement'. By this description they mean that through allowing himself to be put to death in this manner, Jesus somehow 'atoned' for the sins of all of us, and so made it possible for any of us, through faith in him, to be 'at one' with God.

I believe this to be true. I also believe that through letting himself be crucified to his death, completely innocent of any crime though he was, Jesus made it possible for any one who might choose to do so to enter into a new life-giving relationship with God. The Bible describes it as being reconciled with God.

When I attempt to define what is meant by Atonement, I find this endeavour far from either easy or simple. A great number of books have been written on the subject, and a great many words have been spoken; and a great many minds have wrestled long and hard with the problem.

Many ways have been used to explain the Atonement, to spell out exactly what it was that the death of Jesus accomplished. The New Testament says simply and positively 'Christ died for our sins' (1 Corinthians 15:3, RSV). In dying on the cross Jesus did something to help our sinful condition; but how precisely that help was brought about is the question that is so difficult to answer. I will outline some of the answers that have commanded most support down the years. Each gives some insight into the truth of the matter:

(1) Some have regarded the death of Jesus, and his Resurrection which followed, as a great cosmic battle between the forces of evil and the forces of good, whose outcome was a resounding victory for good. The cost was high, but the battle was won; and in this way sin was effectively dealt with.

One very good thing about this explanation is that it keeps the death and resurrection of Jesus close together, when so often they are in danger of being kept apart in some people's thinking. It is important to be aware that Calvary and Easter are not so much separate events as different parts of the one event. Without the Resurrection of Jesus, the world would never have heard of his Crucifixion.

Given this reading of what the death of Jesus effected, the point is made that by means of his death (and Resurrection), Jesus won a resounding victory over sin, and over all the things that are a trouble and a threat to men and women, things like illness, pain, sorrow and death.

Undoubtedly there is truth in this interpretation of the significance of the death of Jesus. The question that remains, however, is whether or not it is the whole of the truth.

(2) Another view is to regard the crucifixion as a matter of Jesus alone bearing the burden of the pain and the punishment which, by rights, belong to every single one of us on account of our sinfulness—in other words, to regard the crucifixion as Jesus presenting himself on the cross as a kind of substitute in place of us.

In this interpretation God is thought of as the great and righteous Judge, whose righteousness leaves him no option but to condemn all men and women because of their sinfulness and to sentence them to the severest of penalties. On Calvary Jesus took on himself the penalty that rightly belonged to us.

(3) The death of Jesus as a sacrifice which made up for (that is, *atoned*) human sinfulness is perhaps the same theory in a slightly different form. On the basis of this sacrifice it became possible for a perfect God to forgive the sins of men and women without denying or impairing his perfection. On one hand God's love wanted men and women to be saved, and on the other hand his own utter righteousness made it impossible for him simply to ignore or condone human sin. This was God's dilemma. When Jesus—who was completely sinless—offered himself as a sacrifice for human sin, this resolved God's dilemma and made it possible for him to forgive sin without doing any despite to his holiness.

There is plainly much truth in these related theories and certainly a great deal that countless people have found inspiring and helpful. There are, however, some questions raised by them to which some attention must be paid.

It might be reckoned, for one thing, that the above theories seem to relegate the love of God to a lesser position than the New Testament affords it. The New Testament emphasises over and over again that the whole process of salvation finds it origin in God's love for his undeserving creatures. For example, we read in Romans 5:8 (RSV), 'God shows his love for us in that while we were yet sinners Christ died for us'. The above theories may appear to suggest, however, that God needed to be *persuaded* to be forgiving towards sinful mankind. That, of course, is not at all how Jesus reveals God's nature to be.

God's nature is love—Jesus makes that abundantly clear. Because of that nature God loves all mankind; and is ever anxious to forgive them their sins. The stumbling-block, so far as God's forgiveness is concerned, is never that of God needing to be cajoled into a forgiving attitude; the stumbling-block is always the reluctance of this man or that woman to seek and to accept the forgiveness made freely available through Jesus Christ.

Some people even feel that these kinds of theories suggest that salvation is obtained for us by dint of God acting in a quite unfair manner, punishing someone completely innocent in order to divert punishment from the guilty.

None of the above theories, therefore, is perfectly straightforward in its endeavour to explain just how it was that the death of Jesus secured salvation for mankind. But they emphasise that something tremendous was accomplished through that death.

(4) Another version of the Atonement theory is to look on the process of salvation as 'redemption' in a quite literal sense, that is, a 'buying back'. The crucifixion was the price that was required to be paid in order to purchase back from the devil a mankind which, wilfully choosing

to go astray, had put itself out of God's possession and into the devil's.

(5) It is extremely difficult to arrive at a clear-cut comprehensive explanation of the Atonement that will satisfy all the features of the death of Jesus on the cross. But whatever the complete explanation might be, there is no doubt that the crucifixion of Jesus demonstrates clearly and unmistakably God's great love for mankind.

Whatever theory or theories we may favour, and however feebly we may understand the meaning of Jesus's crucifixion, one thing is sure and wonderful: that 'it was for us he hung and suffered there'. Whatever else that crucifixion may say, it shouts loud and clear that there was and is no limit to God's love, no lengths beyond which that love would not go on our behalf.

'God so loved the world that he gave up his only son.'

6
I believe in the Love of God

I BELIEVE in the Love of God. I believe in the love of God because I believe in Jesus. I believe that God is a loving God because I believe that God is like Jesus; and Jesus showed unmistakably that God is love. Since Jesus was and is concerned for the welfare of man and women, I am quite sure that this is how it is with God. I have no doubt at all that he is a caring God, because Jesus, his supreme revealer, is a caring Saviour.

At the same time, I am aware that many people find it difficult to share my view because of the existence of suffering—and so much of it—in the world. The fact of suffering raises for them some very pointed and very agonising questions which seem to their minds to deny the existence of a loving God. If I am to hold to my belief that God is love, I must face up to these questions as honestly as I can; and that is what I will now attempt to do.

(1) How, they may say, can we believe that God is a loving God when we see him sending such suffering into human lives?

My answer is that God does *not* send suffering into human lives, at least not in the way they are suggesting he does. Knowing God as he is made known in Jesus, makes it, I believe, impossible to think of him as being that kind of agent of human suffering. I must admit, however, that many people do regard God in that sort of fashion. They believe that every single thing that comes their way is definitely and deliberately wished on them by God.

I myself can think of many instances of this. Mrs Thomson was one. A good Christian and a faithful member of the church for many years, she had a sunny disposition and really enjoyed life. Then came disaster. Her husband died of cancer and two months later her only son was fatally injured.

She was bitterly angry with God and nothing I could say made any difference. 'I don't want anything to do with a God who would treat me like that,' she told me.

Mrs Whitmore was different. She experienced a similar kind of double tragedy but faced up to it with courage and serenity. When I said to her, 'You are taking this marvellously,' she replied, 'Well, it is God's will for me and I must make the best of it'.

These women reacted so differently to their suffering. And yet both, I believe, were equally wrong in thinking that God had chosen to inflict their trouble on them.

He does not sit at some gigantic celestial desk, deciding to parcel out these trials to me and that affliction to you. Whatever troubles come our way are not God's will for us in the sense of his deliberate wish.

Indeed to say he would choose to have a young wife widowed or a boy blinded or a girl raped is to make God into some kind of monster far different from the loving father Jesus makes known to us.

Look at it this way. When a member of the family gets hurt or takes ill, do we sit back and say, 'It is God's will'? Are we not much more likely to send at once for the ambulance or for the doctor? Surely we do not regard ourselves as fighting against the will of God when we do so. Nor do we think of the doctor as opposing God when he tries to make sick people well again, which is what he spends his whole working life doing.

The New Testament supports our opinion. It is made clear there that when Jesus was on earth he did not regard suffering and illness and sorrow as the will of God. He looked upon these things as undesirable and spent a great deal of his limited time doing away with them, healing the sick and comforting the sad.

The plain fact is that Jesus could not have acted like that if he had believed these things to be God's will for the people concerned.

God does not *send* our troubles upon us. We are part of a world where such things may happen and often do.

Sometimes they happen as the result of some calamity of nature, like an earthquake or a fire or a flood. This being a world of natural law, there are times when the processes of that law lead to some kind of natural catastrophe.

Sometimes, again, human suffering is the result of human folly or human evil. And it is not always by any means the guilty—and the guilty alone—who suffer. In other words, the fact is that the bulk of woes which are encountered by mankind can be traced back ultimately to some individual's mistake or sin.

There are other human troubles which I, for one, would not know how to begin to explain. But I am sure of one thing: because of the New Testament's testimony to Jesus, God does not wish our troubles upon us. And when they come, as come they do, his heart bleeds for us, and he is anxious to help us.

It may seem more than a little odd to say—as I am saying—that things may therefore happen to us which God does not really want to happen. This does not appear to say very much for his power and authority.

The situation is, however, that God's omnipotence is voluntarily restricted by the demands of his love.

Undesirable things, or at least their possibility, must be allowed so that his purposes of love may have scope to work themselves out. In other words, God does not *send* suffering in the sense I have been discussing; rather he permits its possibility and allows that possibility to become actuality when the conditions lead to it.

For example, suppose a man is driving his car, his reflexes blurred by alcohol, when a child darts across his path. God permits that child to be struck, perhaps seriously hurt or even killed. He does not decree the happening; but when human folly combines with natural law to produce a certain result, no matter how appalling, he permits it.

To do otherwise would be to cancel out the order of the world and put anarchy in its place. And what would life be like if we could never be sure that solid objects like roads and pavements would remain solid, or whether other solid objects would fall up or down.

You may object—some do—that individuals have found comfort in the face of suffering and sorrow in the belief that this was God's will for them. This is true and I myself know many who have found comfort in this way.

Nevertheless it is, I believe, unlikely that anyone can find the deepest or the most enduring kind of comfort in what is at best only a half truth. The person who finds comfort in believing that God has decreed his or her suffering would surely find much more comfort in recognising that God, far from sending that suffering, is both sharing it with him and offering him help to face it.

What is more, in at least as many instances, great distress has been caused, often leading to abandonment of faith, by the belief that some catastrophe or other is the 'gift' of God.

Here is a man, say, who is drawing strength to endure his suffering from his belief that God has wished it on him. I certainly would not think of telling him in the very context of his personal trial that he had the wrong slant on things. That would be like knocking away a crutch that was at the moment essential to his stability.

The height of a storm is no time for carrying out roof repairs; but if we put our roof to rights in the sunshine, we will be better able to meet the rain and the wind when they come.

Many years ago, I sat at a hospital bed beside a friend who had lost a limb after a road accident. I still remember the radiance of his face when, in response to my murmured sympathy, he said, 'Don't be upset for me. I know this is God's will and I am happy to accept it'.

His faith greatly moved me, but the theology appals me still. He was really making God out to be on a much lower plane than most ordinary men.

The truth is that God 'will never cause his child a needless tear' and any suffering we may have to undergo is actually at variance with his deliberate wish for us. To realise this is to be better equipped to find that strength and courage, which God is most anxious to supply, to meet suffering successfully.

(2) Why, they may now say, does God *allow* all this suffering? If God is as loving as you maintain, why does he not eliminate all pain and sorrow from human experience? Why does he permit such things to befall us?

Laura Richards wrote a fable, called *The Stars*, which tells of a little boy waking up in the night and beginning to cry because, 'I am afraid of the dark, daddy. Why isn't it sunshine all the time?'

Grown men have been asking the same kind of question ever since speech and thought began. Why does the world contain so much that is dark? Why can't human life be lived always in the sunshine?

Why, in other words, does God permit mankind to suffer? This question is especially acute for a Christian believer like myself. The *fact* of suffering is universal: its *problem* is particularly for people such as I.

After all, if I do not believe in God, or if I believe in a malevolent or uncaring supreme power, there is no real problem for me in accepting the existence of suffering.

But since I believe that God is love, I have a problem both real and acute. Why does he allow suffering? Why, indeed, did he make a world where such a thing occurs?

The Bible never takes up this problem in a propositional way. But it implies all the way through that this world is the best possible context for God's purposes of love. And this is how it must be if the New Testament is correct in depicting God as the loving father of Jesus.

Many, however, find this difficult to reconcile with the world as they see it, and human life as they know it. What about that innocent child who is cruelly and senselessly beaten to death? What about that young mother dying of cancer? What about that terrible plane crash?

If God is both loving and all-powerful, why did he not make the world a place where no one need ever suffer? This is the question Browning asked in 'Mihrab Shah':

> *'Wherefore should any evil hap to man—*
> *From ache of flesh to agony of soul—*
> *Since God's All-mercy make All-potency?*
> *Nay, why permits He evil to Himself—*
> *Man's sin accounted such? Suppose a world*
> *Purged of all pain, with fit inhabitant—*
> *Man pure of evil in thought, word and deed—*
> *Were it not well? Then, wherefore otherwise?'*

Many people are inclined to feel that, like Omar Khayyam, in the 'Rubeiyat of Omar Khayyam', they would like:

> *'To grasp this sorry scheme of things entire*
> *. . . Shatter it to bits, and then*
> *Remould it nearer to the heart's desire.'*

The Christian, on the other hand, since he or she accepts the New Testament teaching that God loves us all, must believe that the world God created is the kind best suited to benefit mankind.

This view, it is true, is not always easy to accept, especially when we learn of some new disaster or find ourselves involved in some personal calamity.

Of course, there is another side to the picture. In addition to the suffering that is in the world, there is much that is lovely and happy. Most people in fact find life enjoyable and are reluctant to leave it.

So, when we stop and wonder if God could not have made a better job of the world, we have to be clear as to what exactly we mean by 'better'. We cannot just reckon this up in terms of our being happy or free from trouble.

It is not that these things are unimportant, nor that God is disinterested in them. But there is more to it than that. Christians believe that this world is not the whole story of a man's life—not even the main part of it. It is, if you like, the preparation for what is to follow. This world matters a great deal. But it is not everything. And we ought not to judge it simply in terms of how free from suffering our lives happen to be.

His loving purposes of fitting us for a destiny beyond this life meant that God had to make the world as it is, carrying in it the risk of pain and sorrow. He could not have left out the possibility of suffering without making it a quite different place.

Let me explain what I mean another way. I am very fond of soccer. Lots of people, men *and* women, are. Millions turn to it for recreation and enjoyment. Soccer is governed by laws that have been devised to make it as good a game as possible; but accidents do happen. Many minor injuries are sustained; sometimes there are serious injuries; occasionally a man has died.

In spite of this, men still play the game, enjoy playing it and want to keep on playing it. The rules, no doubt, could be changed to eliminate the risk of injury. But that would make it a different game and, most would think, a poorer one.

God, for his part, could no doubt have made a world free from the risk of suffering. But would this have made it a *better* world, that is, a world better suited for our growth?

For one thing, he could not have eliminated suffering without also eliminating free-will. If we are given freedom of choice, there must always be the danger that we may cause hurt to ourselves and to others. Yet free choice is necessary to the development of our personality.

For another thing, God, omnipotent though he is, cannot be expected to do absurd or self-contradictory things, like striking a match on a bar of soap. Likewise he cannot fashion free human personalities without allowing them free-will.

It is, you see, not because he does not care, but because he *does*, that God has given us free-will and the attendant risk of suffering.

It is for the same reason that he does not interfere with the natural laws that govern the world, even though their operation leads at times to human suffering. It is not because he cannot, but because he must not.

If I step out in front of a bus which is travelling at speed, I am likely to meet with serious injury because God will not arrest its movement in order to save me from being hurt.

To do that kind of thing would be to make nonsense of life. Chaos and anarchy would take over from law and order—life would become virtually unlivable.

Suppose I have a child who has just reached the toddling stage. I love him dearly and I do not want him to be hurt. At the same time, I want him to develop into the

man he is meant to be; and so, for starters, I want him to
learn to walk. When, therefore, he begins to take the first
faltering steps on his own, I permit him, with all the
accompanying risks for the present and for the future. I
let him walk—and perhaps fall—not because I do not
care for him enough, but because I do.

Likewise God lets us run the risk of suffering, not
because he does not love us, but because he does. And
when that risk becomes a fact, he loves us still. Paul, in the
face of much personal suffering, was so sure of this that he
was able to write: 'I am convinced that there is nothing in
death or in life, nothing in all creation that can separate us
from the love of God in Christ Jesus our Lord'.

(3) Another question that is often posed agonisingly, and
just as often felt as such, is this: 'How can you believe in
a loving God when life is so unfair at times, punishing
the innocent and letting the guilty go scot-free?'

This question is based on the assumption that suffering is, or is meant to be, a punishment for wrong-doing;
but that is an assumption that has to be challenged. Many
people do look on suffering as punishment for sin. Life,
they reckon, simply gives us what we deserve. And they
sometimes use scripture to back their conviction. It is
certainly the opinion put forward time and again in the
earlier Old Testament days. The people of Israel believed
firmly that God punished evil and rewarded good.

The Psalms give expression many times to this point
of view. In Psalm 128 it says, 'Blessed is everyone who
fears the Lord, who walks in his ways! You shall eat the
fruit of the labour of your hands; you shall be happy, and
it shall be well with you' (RSV). On the other hand,
Psalm 91:8 says, 'You will only look with your eyes and
see the recompense of the wicked' (RSV).

These passages can be paralleled many times in the

Psalms and elsewhere. Goodness is sure to be rewarded, evil is bound to be punished; and all of this will happen in this present world.

At the same time many Psalms take account of the fact that often the wicked do seem to prosper. But in their opinion this is never more than temporary. In the end—it may be sooner, it may be later—punishment catches up with them and suffering comes along in its wake. Psalm 37:1-2, for instance, says, 'Fret not yourself because of the wicked, be not envious of wrong-doers! For they will soon fade like the grass, and wither like the green herb' (RSV). Thus it may appear that the idea which prevails in the Old Testament is that men always get what they deserve. All suffering is God's punishment for wrong-doing.

The book of Job illustrates this widely-held view. However, it is not really the view of the author of Job, nor the teaching of his book. Job is a holy man, God's man, and his prosperity proves it. But suddenly disaster strikes. One calamity follows another, striking at his possessions, his family and his person. When it does, everyone assumes unquestioningly that this must be the consequence of some sin that he has committed.

His friends say to him, 'What terrible thing have you done to deserve such punishment as this?' Job emphatically denies that he has committed any such awful sin. Their assumptions are misguided. He insists that he is just as much a man of God now as he ever was in the days when everything went well with him. At the conclusion the book repudiates the assumption that Job's suffering must have been a punishment for his sin. At the same time it reveals how widespread that assumption was. And in New Testament times, the same assumption still prevailed.

This is illustrated, for instance, when Jesus and his disciples encounter a man who has been blind from birth.

The disciples ask, 'Rabbi, who sinned, this man or his parents, that he was born blind?' (John 9:1-2, RSV). They take it for granted that where there is affliction, there must have been some sin for which this is the punishment.

This notion is far from dead even yet. You may well have heard said what most ministers have heard many times—'What have I done to merit this?' or 'Why should so-and-so have this to suffer? They have done nothing to deserve it'.

Many people cling to this idea that whether or not you suffer is a matter of deserts, with God dispensing punishment to the evil-doers and blessing to the righteous. It is an idea, however, which cannot legitimately survive in the face of the facts. As Stanley Jones has stated, 'It is simply not true that earthquakes hit the bad and spare the good. An earthquake in India shook down a mission building and left a brothel standing nearby'.

Jesus certainly would have none of this view of suffering, either in the incident quoted above, or anywhere else for that matter.

Not that he offers any other explanation. Even the closest scrutiny of the New Testament will fail to reveal any theory of suffering sponsored by Jesus. He does not see it as any part of his mission to explain why suffering exists.

The chief problem is not, in any case, its why, but its how: that is, *how* to overcome it. In this respect Jesus certainly does have an answer. He does not offer to explain human suffering, but he does offer to help us overcome it. 'In the world you have tribulation; but be of good cheer, I have overcome the world' (John 16:33, RSV).

This is of much greater importance. After all, even if a full explanation of suffering were available, its real problem—that of how to come through it triumphantly —would still be with us. In the end this is the only question that really matters.

Let us suppose that I am lying in hospital, smashed up after a car accident; and let us suppose that I understand it all perfectly—I have still to contend with the fact that I am lying in that hospital bed smashed up.

Or let us suppose that I am a sailor caught up in a storm at sea; and let us suppose that I understand exactly how the various factors of the wind and temperature and the rest have combined to produce that storm. That knowledge does not deliver me from the storm. I need something more than that to enable me to ride it out successfully.

It is the 'something more' that Jesus offers to provide in the face of the storms of life. He does not claim to unravel the mysteries of human suffering. Nor does he promise to keep us free from it. His promise is, 'When trials come upon you, as come they will, remember that I am by your side and anxious to help you'.

In conclusion, then, I believe that God is a God of love because Jesus has made it so abundantly plain that he is. Faith in Jesus Christ does not guarantee our escape from suffering—far from it—but it does guarantee us his help in facing it. He will, in fact, keep us safe and secure even though we lose everything in the world, even though we lose our very lives.

It has been known to happen that in a gale, a bird may be blown from his tree-top perch. This must be a terrifying experience for the poor bird. But it is not—or need not be, at any rate—final disaster for him. He has his wings and with them he can make a safe landing.

The storms of life will sometimes blow the Christian about very frighteningly. But he has the wings of his faith.

7

I believe in the Justice of God

I BELIEVE that God is just. This does not mean, however, that I subscribe to the view that God dispenses strict justice to every man and every woman, giving them exactly what they deserve, no more no less. Some people, it is true, do hold this opinion and would maintain that everything that befalls us is either a reward for righteousness or a punishment for wrong-doing.

I believe that this point of view is clearly irreconcilable with the actual facts of human experience. At the same time I must admit that it is an idea which is continually met in the Old Testament, particularly in the earlier books.

The people of Israel believed firmly that God punished evil-doing and rewarded good works. In Deuteronomy 11:26-28, for instance, we find this: 'I offer you the choice of a blessing and a curse. The blessing will come if you listen to the commandments of the Lord your God' (NEB). We meet the very same idea in, to take another example, Jeremiah 17:5: 'These are the words of the Lord: A curse on the man who trusts in man and leans for support on humankind while his heart is far from the Lord! . . . Blessed is the man who trusts in the Lord, and rests his confidence upon him' (NEB).

Such passages as these—and there are many, many more—unmistakably represent the view that God invariably and inevitably punishes evil and rewards good.

This dispensation of rewards and punishments was, in the Old Testament view, entirely fulfilled in this world. This, of course, was how it had to be, so far as they could see. Most of the Old Testament has no thought of life beyond this world. It was only very late on in the Old Testament period that any vision of the life hereafter began to be glimpsed, and even then only in fragments.

So, then, I am forced to concede that the characteristic and predominant view of the people of the Old Testament was that a just God assigned weal or woe to men and women in this life strictly according to their merits or demerits.

The dominant idea of the Hebrews was that men and women always got what they deserved. Everything that comes to us is meted out to us by God according to the kind of person we have shown ourselves to be and the kind of lives we have led.

Frequently in our day the underlying assumption many people adopt towards life is that trouble and freedom from trouble, success and lack of success, are matters that God deals out to individuals strictly in accordance with their deserts—punishment for the evil-doer and blessing for the well behaved.

It must be admitted that there *is* a retributive quality about many of the world's woes and much of human suffering. Wrong-doing often does produce consequences of pain and misery. Here, for instance, is someone who has contracted a disease that is directly traceable to their sexual promiscuity. Here is another who has fallen victim to cirrhosis of the liver and it is directly traceable to drinking to excess over a period of many years. Here is yet another whose very successful business has collapsed in ruins and this catastrophe is directly traceable to an increasing attention to selfish pleasures accompanied by an increasing neglect of business affairs.

The world in which we live in many ways is a moral world in which, naturally and inevitably, wickedness brings punishment and goodness brings reward. But when

I affirm that I believe in God's justice, I do not mean simply that he has created a world of a moral nature. To leave it there would be to represent God's justice as hard and unfeeling—somewhat akin to the nature of Shylock's insistence on his pound of flesh.

It is beyond doubt that much of the world's woe is the direct result of human error and sin. But it is far from being an inflexible rule that the guilty suffer in this life and the innocent prosper. This is patently not the case. Here, for instance, is a man who all his days has lived a clean and wholesome life; he is struck down by a cancer which takes him, after prolonged pain, to an early grave. Here is a woman who is of the sweetest temper and the kindest disposition; a severe coronary attack lays her low at a comparatively early age.

I do not believe that God's justice means that to every person he metes out a pound of punishment in return for a pound of wrong-doing, cr a pound of blessing in return for a pound of good behaviour. How can I, when quite clearly many people do *not* get what they would seem to deserve, not in this world at least?

Some people would take this evident fact to prove that God, far from being just, is not even fair. My belief is that God indeed is not strictly fair: God, I believe, is *more* than fair. His justice is intermingled with his mercy.

Jesus told a parable which outlines this very message. It is the story of the 'labourers in the vineyard' (Matthew 20:1-16, RSV). A vineyard owner was in need of additional casual labour at the time of the grape harvest in order to have the grapes gathered in before the rains came. As was customary, he went to the marketplace at the beginning of the working day (6 am) and hired as many extra hands as were available. He hired them at the agreed (and regular) rate of one denarius for the day's work. Still in need of further assistance, he paid repeated visits to the marketplace as the day advanced; and continued to take on additional labour right up to the hour before the day's end, promising only that he would give the later starters a fair payment.

At the end of the day (6 pm), all the day labourers lined up to receive their wages—and to the surprise of all everyone received one denarius. Those who had started to work at 6 am complained that their employer, in paying the same wage to those who had worked only for part of the day, was being unfair to those who had worked for the whole day. The owner answered that he had been perfectly fair to them, having paid them in full the agreed wage; and he had chosen to be more than fair to the others and to give them more than they had really earned.

The point was not that he had given the early starters only what he gave the late starters; the point was that he had given the late starters as much as he had given the early starters. And in each case it was the *full* day's wage.

God, the parable is saying, is like that. His love knows no bounds and, therefore, justice is not a matter of dispensing to all exactly what they deserve. Otherwise no one would be saved. God gives the very utmost he has to give to everyone who is willing to receive it. He cannot give more than everything his love has to bestow; and he does not want any one of us to be content with less.

And thus my belief in the justice of God is synonymous with my belief in the generosity of his love.

8
I believe in the Miracles of Jesus

I BELIEVE that Jesus performed miracles. I find the evidence that he did so too strong to be set aside. The case for believing in the miracles of Jesus strikes me as being overwhelming.

I am well aware that the Gospels, which are our record of Jesus and his miracles, were written by Christians, by people who thought the world of him and who may, therefore, with every justification, be considered strongly biased in his favour. Nevertheless, their testimony that Jesus could and did work miracles cannot reasonably be resisted.

The very fact that his companions thought so highly of him and were utterly convinced that he had unique powers which were often translated into miraculous action, in itself a testimony to the reality of these unique powers. They believed that he could and did accomplish miracles because they had so often witnessed him doing so. Even if you agree that they might at times have misunderstood or misinterpreted what they saw Jesus do, you can in no way disregard the overall effect the deeds of Jesus had upon them. He must have been, beyond any shadow of doubt, a very special person. And he must have done some very special things to have produced in his close friends and companions the deep impression they gained that he was able to perform miraculous deeds and often, in fact, did just that.

Not only that, there are so many miracles recorded in the Gospels, and there were so many witnesses to most of them, some of whom were very hard-headed types and not at all of a credulous disposition. These facts, too, make it extremely difficult to write off the reports of the miracles of Jesus as misguided flights of fancy or anything like that.

The Gospels make it perfectly plain to me that Jesus was a person possessed of remarkable powers, who performed a whole lot of remarkable deeds that demand to be described as miraculous, a miracle being something that at the time of its occurrence is beyond the capacity of human knowledge, skill or power to achieve. On the basis of that definition there is no room in my mind for doubt concerning the proposition that Jesus worked miracles —and not merely as occasional special tricks, but as a regular feature of his ministry.

That is not to say that I would insist that every miracle reported in the New Testament happened exactly as it is described therein. On the contrary, I am perfectly willing to admit that there may have been times when the disciples of Jesus misunderstood some of those things they had witnessed Jesus do. They became so accustomed to this extraordinary leader of theirs bringing about extraordinary things that, at times, they may well have put two and two together and come up with the answer of five, or even six!

What I am trying to say is this: I believe in the miracles of Jesus and I believe that he could have performed every recorded miracle exactly as it may appear at first sight. But I recognise at the same time that it is right and proper—and necessary—to examine each miracle carefully and thoroughly on its own, in order to determine as far as we can what exactly took place; and at the same time to assess why it was selected for inclusion in the limited space of the Gospel record, and also what lesson it may have to teach us today.

Take the calming of the storm as an example. The narrative tells us that on one occasion Jesus was sailing in a boat with his disciples on the Sea of Galilee when suddenly a violent storm erupted around them. This was a fairly common experience on the Sea of Galilee—as a matter of fact it still is—and frequently these storms could be frighteningly dangerous.

It was just this kind of storm that descended upon the boat carrying Jesus and his disciples that day. The little craft tossed and turned and threatened to sink; the disciples were panic-stricken. Jesus, whose day had been particularly exhausting, lay asleep in the stern of the boat. The disciples rushed to him in their terror and woke him up: 'We're in danger of sinking!' they cried. 'Do you not care for our safety?' Jesus, the story goes on, stood up and calmed the storm. The wind dropped, the waves subsided, sailing became smooth once more; and the panic in the hearts of the disciples was quietened.

I would not claim to know precisely what occurred on the Sea of Galilee on that dramatic afternoon. I have no doubt that Jesus had the power to calm the storm, literally and physically—and it may be that this was exactly what he did. It may be however, as some would suggest is more likely, that Jesus allowed the storm to take its course, but at the same time calmed the other storm, the storm of fear that was raging in the hearts of his followers.

I do not know for sure the details of the miracle Jesus performed on the Sea of Galilee that day, but I have no doubt that he did something very wonderful. That is how it is for me with more than one of the recorded miracles of Jesus. I know beyond doubt that a miracle was performed, but I do not know for sure just what was done.

The feeding of the five thousand is another instance. I cannot explain how it was done, but I believe firmly that one day on the shores of that same Sea of Galilee, Jesus was able to satisfy the physical hunger of thousands of people using only five small loaves and two little fishes.

It is another familiar story. Jesus had been preaching and healing on the north-west shore of the lake. He decided to cross over by boat, with his disciples, to the opposite shore, hoping, it would appear, to get a little time to himself in order to recharge his spiritual batteries. The vast crowd to whom he had been speaking divined his intention and also managed to estimate pretty accurately the destination he had in mind. So they set off by foot and in haste around the northern end of the coast and arrived before the boat did—not at all surprising, particularly if there happened to be a contrary wind, which would make rowing for the disciples not only more laborious, but also much slower.

Although no doubt disappointed at this rather unexpected turn of events, Jesus with his characteristic compassion set about ministering to the gathering. Not content with that, Jesus then refused to disperse the crowd to fend for themselves so far as food was concerned. Instead, worried about the hunger they must now be feeling after a long day without food, Jesus wanted to do something to help.

His disciples were dismayed and perhaps a little angry. 'How can you or we do anything to help?' they protested. 'Even if we had enough money, where could we purchase sufficient food in this isolated region to satisfy the hunger of these thousands?'

Jesus did not argue with them. He simply asked, 'What food do we have available?' There was a lad there, he was told, who was willing to donate the five rolls and two small fish he was carrying with him—perhaps the picnic lunch a caring and thoughtful mother had furnished him with in order to see him through the day. 'It's ludicrous,' the disciples said, 'to think that such a small amount of food could even begin to solve our problem.'

'Give it to me,' Jesus replied, 'it will be enough.' And,

astonishingly enough, it was. Jesus took the rolls and the
fish and shared them out—with remarkable consequences.
Not only did everyone get enough to eat, but not less than
twelve basketfuls of scraps were collected afterwards.

Once again I have to confess that I do not know exactly
what happened. I cannot explain how it was that Jesus was
able, with such a limited supply of food, to satisfy the hunger
of so many—and yet I believe that somehow he did.

It may well be that Jesus miraculously increased the
physical volume of the loaves and fishes to such an
extent that everyone there had enough to eat and some to
spare. This is how the miracle has traditionally been
understood and I for my part have no difficulty in believing that Jesus possessed such unique powers that he
could have done exactly that.

Whether or not that is how he performed the miracle
may be open to question. Some commentators, at any rate,
suggest that it may not have been a miracle of loaves and
fishes being multiplied in the physical sense, but a miracle
of another kind—changing the attitudes of men and
women. Instead of miraculously transforming loaves and
fishes, Jesus miraculously transformed human hearts.

In other words, Jesus was well aware that the majority
of those who made up that vast crowd had been prudent
and foresighted enough to provide for themselves and
their kin, like the little lad's mother, and carried food
with them on what was obviously going to be a long
journey and an even longer day. And as that day drew
near its close, they would be hungry and more than ready
to delve into their provisions. But people tend to be
basically selfish and perhaps they hesitated to produce
their food in case their neighbours had less or even none
at all. In such a case they might feel compelled to share
with them and so have less for themselves; or else they
might munch away on their own and feel embarrassed at

doing so. When Jesus took the boy's provisions, blessed them and shared them out generously to those around him, it was like opening a floodgate. The force of his loving personality and the impact of his unselfish action swept away the selfishness that had been restraining the crowd. Almost at once, those who had brought food with them took it out and shared it around; and so there was enough and more for all.

I cannot tell exactly how the miracle of calming the storm was accomplished, nor can I say what the mechanics of the feeding of the five thousand might have been. But I have no doubt that Jesus did these marvellous things, and many others as well.

I believe that he also worked a great many miracles of a different kind—miracles of healing. Many were the men and women he healed of all sorts of ailments—physical, mental and spiritual. Jesus mended broken bones and broken hearts and broken lives.

I believe that Jesus can, and still does, work miracles. I believe that his touch has not lost its ancient power. He does not always heal physical diseases nowadays, even when he is asked. In fact, he usually does not. Usually he lets such things run their natural course. He does not as a rule keep his followers free from pain and illness and suffering and trouble. But he has the power to help them face up to these kind of things and to win through them.

Let me return to the calming of the storm on the Sea of Galilee. Whatever exactly happened that day, there is no doubt that Jesus soothed the storms of fear that were raging in the hearts of his disciples. And I believe that Jesus is performing that same kind of miracle today.

I believe in the miracles of Jesus.

I believe in the miracles he performed when on earth.

I believe in the miracles he is performing today.

9

I believe in Prayer

I BELIEVE in prayer. I believe in its efficiency. I believe prayer works. That, however, must not be taken to mean that I believe that I will receive everything and anything I pray for. Prayer is not to be regarded as some kind of magical order form that the divine Santa Claus must and will deliver in full. At the same time, I do believe in prayer and I believe that a sincere prayer is always answered.

I will return to that latter thought, but first I would like to make it plain that asking God to do things is not all there is to prayer. It is not even the major part of it. Prayer is a matter of talking over with God anything that concerns our own lives, the lives of our relatives, friends and acquaintances; the life of the society of which we are part; the life of our country; the life of our world. Prayer has many aspects and many types.

It does include asking of God on our own behalf—this form of prayer is usually termed Petition. It also includes, for instance, asking things for others (Intercession); seeking forgiveness for wrong-doing (Confession); simply having conversation with one who knows and understands and cares (Communion); praising God in acknowledgment of his greatness (Adoration); asking his help in the business of living generally, or in the facing of some situation in particular (Supplication).

There are many misunderstandings about Prayer. One of the most common is, perhaps, to think of it as a one-way street, all a matter of talking to God and God listening to us in return. Prayer, however, in its full and intended dimension, is a two-way street process. Not only is it a case of our speaking to a listening God; it is also a case of God speaking to our listening souls.

Frequently, to our spiritual impoverishment, we make our prayers into constant monologues where we talk incessantly and never take time to listen to the 'still, small voice' of God. Ordinary human experience is, of course, often very similar. I have encountered instance after instance of this during my pastoral visits, as have most people in their day to day activities.

Many a time I have left a house with the occupant saying to me, in all obvious sincerity, 'Thank you for our lovely conversation, I enjoyed it so much and I feel so much the better for it', when, in fact, he or she had done practically all the talking with hardly a break for breath, never mind listening to any response I might have wanted to make.

Frequently that is just what our prayers are like. We do all the talking and make no time—often have no desire—for listening. But prayer that is only a monologue is prayer that is only part of what it is meant to be. We are meant to give God the opportunity to put in a word at least now and then.

Another common misunderstanding about prayer is to regard it as a sort of chore which God imposes on us as a kind of discipline which we must attend to with diligence in order to keep him in good humour. The fact is that prayer is for our benefit, and not for God's pleasure.

Far from being the irksome obligation some regard it, prayer is in reality an astonishing privilege. It means that at any time any one of us may enter into conversation with the Supreme Being. Most people would count it an opportunity to be greatly treasured if they were permitted to have a private audience with the chief person of their country—the Queen, the King, the President, or whoever it might be—and would be anxious to make the most of it.

What is offered in prayer is an opportunity to have an audience with the King of Kings.

This is an opportunity that is available at all times, and it may well be that this very fact leads to an apparent devaluation of it in the eyes and minds of many. Familiarity may sometimes tend to blur the exceptional privilege that prayer affords, the freedom to have conversation with the Almighty whenever we choose.

If we were allowed a time of prayer only once or twice a year, say, what a difference that might make to the attitude of a great many people towards it and their appreciation of it. Most of us would be waiting in a fever of impatience for the next permitted time of prayer to arrive so that we might get talking to God.

Yet another common misapprehension about prayer is somehow to regard it as a means of persuading God to adopt a certain line of action, something that perhaps he would rather not do, but concerning which he might yield a point if sufficient pressure is exerted on him through prayer.

The function of this kind of (Petitionary) prayer, the making of petitions or requests to God, is not in the least like that. Prayer is not a tool of coercion placed in our hands so that we might use it to wrestle concessions from a reluctant God.

A glorious truth made crystal clear in Jesus is that God loves us and desires the very best for us without our needing to ask him. He has, however, given us the gift of freedom of choice and he does not, therefore—*must* not indeed—force anything upon us against our will, no matter how good. He constantly desires to assist us to live our lives to the best and to the full; but he must wait for our willingness to receive that assistance before he can give it to us. Prayer is one of the means within our power that may be used to make it possible for the loving

God to give us a greater measure of the assistance he always wishes to give but never compels us to accept unwillingly.

In this aspect of its function and its potential, prayer is rather like a supply line along which God can, if we are agreeable, convey his helpfulness (his 'grace') into our lives. Our part in this operation is to maintain that supply line by keeping it in regular use.

If, on entering a room, I depress the light switch and the room is at once flooded with light, that does not mean that I have persuaded the electricity to transform itself reluctantly into illumination. What I have done is to effect the completion of the circuit which is necessary to permit the power, already present and prepared, to realise its potential and become light. That may be taken as a rough analogy of what is accomplished by prayer in one of its capacities.

Is prayer necessary? Since God knows everything about us and always desires the best for us anyway, it may well be asked if there is any point in saying prayers to him. But the point is that God can rarely do all that he would like to do for us without our co-operation, and prayer is one means of giving him that co-operation.

When, then, should prayer be used? The answer to this question is that prayer should be employed at any time and at every time. It is not something to be reserved for special occasions and used only rarely. It is meant for regular and for everyday use. It is most certainly not something that is kept in reserve for emergencies only.

I well remember many years ago a girl in my Youth Fellowship saying to me with, if not exactly horror in her voice, certainly distaste and astonishment, 'I have a workmate who says prayers *every day*'. Beyond any doubt she regarded her colleague as decidedly odd.

Many people have the same sort of idea about the

frequency with which prayer is to be used. Even a considerable number of faithful church members appear to look on prayer as if it were clearly marked 'for emergency use only'.

I recall, for instance, one occasion when I was making a hospital visit to one of my church elders. As I came to the end of my visit I asked him, as was my custom, 'Would you like me to offer a short prayer?' His reaction was an immediate, 'No, I'm not as ill as that'. As it happens his illness was terminal, but in any event prayer is not valid only in the major crises of life. It is for regular daily use and is meant to help us through the lesser crises and the ordinary days as well.

Not only is prayer intended for everyday use, it is something for everyone to use. A man once said to me, 'I never say prayers. Prayer is not my cup of tea'. But prayer can be anybody's cup of tea and is for everybody without exclusion or distinction. It does not require special skills or a particular temperament. Although it can be worked at so that we can learn to use it more and more *effectively*, it is, basically, a simple matter of talking with someone who knows us and understands us and cares for us. That understanding and caring someone—God—may be depended upon to hear and to answer our every prayer.

There is, let me repeat, no such thing as an unanswered prayer. God, it is true, will not always do exactly what we ask or give us precisely what we request. Sometimes he may say 'No' (after all, he knows much better than we do what is ultimately best for us) or 'not yet' or 'not in the way you wish' or 'not at the time you are choosing'. But even when he must refuse the immediate request, he always answers the underlying desire.

God never fails to answer the person who makes a sincere request. When, as will usually be the case, he must not change the circumstances which are troubling us, he will always provide the strength and resources that are required in order to enable us to rise triumphant above these circumstances, whatever they happen to be.

Following on a broadcast I had made, I once had a continuing correspondence with an Irish mother of three young boys. One of the boys was ill with leukaemia and their mother told me how every night she prayed this prayer with his brothers: 'Lord, please make Owen better'. One day I received a letter from her in which she informed me that Owen had died. She went on to say, 'At first I did not know what to say that night in our evening prayer and in the end I simply said, "Thank you, Lord, for making Owen better"'.

The terms of her request were not granted, but God, I believe, certainly answered her. And he will just as surely, I believe, answer anyone and everyone who prays to him in sincerity, by giving them the strength and the resources that are needed to see them through whatever crisis may be confronting them.

10
I believe in the Beatitudes

I BELIEVE in the Beatitudes. These are the sayings of Jesus which stand at the beginning of the Sermon on the Mount and are recorded in the opening verses of chapter 5 of St Matthew's Gospel.

I believe in them. That is not simply to say that I believe they were in fact spoken by Jesus. It is also to say that I know that in them Jesus expresses the very essence of the Christian way of life.

There is a place in the Holy Land called the Mount of Beatitudes. I have been there many times. Always, like every other pilgrimage leader, when I am leading a group round the Christian sites in that land, I make a special point of visiting there. It is a singularly beautiful spot, especially in the sunshine which is almost invariably the order of things in the spring and the autumn, the normal seasons for my Holy Land pilgrimages; and it is the place that tradition has assigned to the Lord's preaching of his Sermon on the Mount.

Situated on the north-western shore of the Sea of Galilee, the hill to which the name Mount of Beatitudes has been given is surmounted by the Church of the Beatitudes. A modern Italian church, its cloisters command a superb view of the blue waters of the lake below. Standing there and looking upon the slopes which fall below one's feet to the water's edge, it is not at all difficult to imagine these very slopes crowded with people gathered to hear Jesus preach, as no doubt happened many times.

No one is likely to suggest that Jesus would preach

the whole of the Sermon on the Mount (Matthew, chapters 5-7) on a single occasion. It is evident that Matthew gathered together for convenience in the same section of his Gospel a mass of teaching which Jesus had delivered at different times and probably at different locations.

It is quite likely, however, that much of it may have been given at or around the place we now know as the Mount of Beatitudes. It may well be at any rate that the Beatitudes which open the Sermon on the Mount were actually spoken by Jesus to his disciples at this very spot.

It certainly was, and still is, an ideal place for delivering sermons or lessons in the open air. As visitors can, and often do, test for themselves, the outdoor accoustics are phenomenally good. Someone standing at the water's edge, or a few paces into the sea, can speak in a conversational voice and be heard perfectly clearly by someone standing or sitting well up the hillside.

In any event, the Beatitudes, which are tied so closely by tradition to this particular spot, are tied even more closely to the Christian way of life. They lie at the very heart of Jesus's teaching to his disciples. *To his disciples* —that is worth emphasising.

It is important to stress that the Beatitudes were not general teaching addressed to all and sundry. They were —and still are—instructions to those already committed to Jesus and his way. They are an exposition and an amplification of what it means to follow that way; not a means of admission to it.

This is not always understood. Many times I have heard it said—and I have no doubt that most ministers have had similar experiences—'I do not want any truck with religion; but I do my best to follow the Beatitudes. Surely that is more important'. The fact is, however, that the Beatitudes cannot be divorced from the Christian faith. They have neither relevance nor meaning apart from that faith. The Christian way of life is really possible only for the committed Christian; because the Christian ideal as set forth in the Beatitudes requires the dynamic of Christian faith to make it attainable.

That is why it is of first importance to keep in mind that the Beatitudes were addressed to Christ's disciples. I have heard the opinion expressed that 'what the world needs is not more Christians but more people living out the Beatitudes'. That, however, is a contradiction in terms. It is not possible for anyone to achieve the Christian ethic in any great measure without the Christian religion.

One of the distinctive things about Christianity is that it not only delineates the good life, but also offers to supply the power to achieve it. This is obtained through putting our trust in Jesus and living in friendship with him. That is what Christian belief affirms and I share that belief, because I have seen it proved time and time again.

The ideal of Christian living, the essence of which is concentrated in the Beatitudes, is far beyond anyone's reach without the help of Christ. With that help, however, it is placed within the reach of anyone and of everyone. This is where part of the uniqueness of Christianity resides.

There are other religions and other philosophies which make a fair stab at describing how the good man or woman ought to live; but all of them have to leave it to the individual to strive after that goodness as best he or she can, in their own strength. Jesus Christ, on the other hand, not only gives, I believe, the finest moral teaching ever, he is also able and willing to assist us to live it out.

There is a great deal of hope and encouragement in this for us frail and fallible mortals. It can be depressing and discouraging to have lofty standards of behaviour and conduct set before us, and to know that our own inner resources are insufficient to enable us to attain these standards with any real degree of success and consistency. It can make all the difference to discover that Jesus not only points out the way of living that is best, but can also provide the inspiration and dynamic to follow that way.

It is my belief that he can do this. I believe that the same Jesus who taught the Beatitudes on the shores of Lake Galilee long ago is alive today, and that he is both able and willing to assist all who are prepared to accept his help, to work at these Beatitudes in their lives from day to day.

11

I believe in Heaven

I BELIEVE that beyond this life God has in store for his people another and a better life. I believe in heaven. Not everyone, I am well aware, shares this belief. Some, indeed, would ridicule it, perhaps with as much rancour as Iago in Verdi's opera *Othello*. His 'Credo' aria in that opera makes my scalp prickle every time I hear it.

Iago has been declaiming his creed that, as far as he is concerned, evil is good and good is evil. He goes on to sing: 'What of the good man . . . he plays his part . . . but when the solemn farce is o'er . . . and he goes down to the wormy tomb . . . when death comes . . . what then . . . what then? . . . why, then . . . there's nothing'.

I, for my part, believe that so far from there being nothing after death, there is a new and quite marvellous life which is on offer for the taking, and this offer extends to everyone. And I owe my belief in this to Jesus.

Many people, I know, have had a feeling of being immortal without recourse to the Christian faith. Many have echoed or re-echoed the words of Robert Browning: 'I know this earth is not my sphere. For I can not so narrow me but I still exceed it'. Many people from different cultures and from different ages have felt similar intimations of immortality.

Such intimations could all, of course, be the result of self-delusion. They could be no more than a refusal, prompted perhaps by vanity, to admit that there could be an end to us.

But I believe that there is a life to come not only because of some subjective feelings, but because of Jesus.

He has told us quite plainly—and I am prepared to accept his word on the matter—that there is something more in store. He has said things like, for instance: 'I am the Resurrection and I am Life. If a man has faith in me, even though he die, he shall come to life' (John 11:25, NEB) and 'Set your troubled hearts at rest . . . . There are many dwelling places in my father's house' (John 14:1, 2, NEB).

That is what Jesus has to say about it and that is enough for me. In any case, his words are backed up by his Resurrection from the dead. Whatever else that dramatic event signifies, it is surely a sign and a promise that, as Jesus was raised to life again, so his followers will live again when their earthly lives have run their course. The Christian is assured that death is for him not so much the end of life as the beginning of a new life.

D L Moody, the famous American evangelist of a past generation, once said to a group of his friends, 'Some morning you will pick up the newspaper and you will read in it that D L Moody is dead. When you do, don't believe it. At that moment I will be more alive than I am now'.

That is the Christian belief and I share it.

Many, it must be admitted, find this doctrine difficult to accept. I remember a friend saying to me once, 'How can we be sure there is another life after this one? No one has ever come back to tell us'.

But that is just the point so far as I am concerned. I believe that Jesus has come back and has told us. If we choose not to pay attention to him—and it is, of course, our right thus to choose if we wish—then I believe that we miss out on something important and wonderful and true.

However, I am not suggesting that this is the whole story of what the Christian faith is about. Not in the least.

Following Jesus is not only about getting into heaven when we die. Some Christians, I know, are rightly criticised for appearing to give the impression that this *is* what it is all about. They are 'so heavenly minded as to be no earthly use'. No, the Christian faith is very much to do with *this* world as well as with the next.

At the same time, Christianity does have to do with the next world. Jesus's promise of the life everlasting to his followers is a very important thing. And if this is a promise to be relied on—and I believe it is, since it has the work and words of Jesus to support it—then it is a great pity to ignore it, since it can make a difference even to this present life.

It can, for one thing, make a great difference in the face of bereavement. To know that there is another and a better life to follow this one does not remove the pain of being bereaved, but it can go a long way towards easing that pain and eventually overcoming it. It is a help, for instance, that we are given assurance that our loved ones are not really dead, but, rather, have begun a new life. It helps, too, to have the prospect of reunion in heaven. Where there is a loving relationship, the separation caused by death is inevitably a source of much pain; but the pain may be lessened to some degree by the confident hope of meeting again in the next life.

Belief in the life to come can, and often does, make a great difference in the face of bereavement. It can also make a great difference to the contemplation of the certain fact that we ourselves must someday die. I remember visiting a member of my congregation who was close to death and who knew it. Suddenly she said to me, quietly but firmly, 'Don't be troubled for me. I know that what you preach is true and since my trust is in Jesus, I'm not afraid to die'.

Furthermore, belief in the life everlasting can make a

mighty difference not only to the business of dying but also to the business of living. To know that this world is not the whole story can give life a totally new perspective. It adds meaning and purpose to life in this world when we are aware that there is another life to follow. This provides an incentive to put our every talent and every opportunity to the fullest use.

I believe in the life everlasting and I regard it as one of the great articles of faith of the Christian Church. It has given inspiration for living and serenity in dying to multitudes of Christians .

I remember another of my church members—a man in his eighties—who had been bedridden for many months. Every time I called on him, I would say, 'How are you today?', and always he would reply, 'I'm fine'. One day when I called he was clearly very ill, but when I said my usual, 'How are you today?', back came the usual response, 'I'm fine'.

My face may have shown something of my feelings of concern, for he added almost at once, with a serene smile, 'Don't be worried about me, I have a great future ahead of me'. He died only a few hours later and moved on, I firmly believe, to that great future to which he was referring.

I believe in heaven—but I would not attempt to describe in any detail what heaven is like. There are some, I know, who are much less diffident and who almost give the impression of having such intimate knowledge of heaven that they could, if asked, provide a street map and tourist commentary. The Bible, however, does not reveal heaven to us in such detail. It may speak about heaven many times and may mention, for example, that it has streets of gold. It is clear, however, that the Bible writers on occasions like this are using metaphor and imagery and do not intend us to take such expressions literally.

Even Jesus does not attempt to enlighten us on the details
of what heaven is like.

The main reason for the lack of detail may be that we
would be incapable of grasping the complete picture
anyway. Heaven is life in a different dimension from
what we experience in our present existence; and the
things we are acquainted with here, and the categories we
employ, could never be adequate to describe the new-
dimensional life that is still to unfold.

Think, for instance, of how we frequently speak of
heaven as if it were a place. Now, we are all perfectly
aware that heaven is not a place in the same sense as, say,
Glasgow or London are places, *ie* locations that can be
pin-pointed by latitude and longitude. Nevertheless, because of our necessary limitations of thought and speech,
we continue to use such terms, simply because we find it
so difficult to speak of heaven in any other way. Similarly,
we go on speaking of God in human terms (like 'father'
for instance), even though we are well aware that he is
much more than human and that, therefore, such terms
can never fully describe him. We continue to use such
terms because, although known to be inadequate, they are
nevertheless the best available to us.

It is understandable that we should wish to have further information about heaven than we possess. But,
shackled by our humanity as we are, we must remain for
the most part ignorant of the nature of heaven until we
actually get there. Then there will be all the thrill of glad
discovery. This no doubt was in the forefront of Sir
James Barrie's mind when he had Peter Pan say, 'To die
will be an awfully great adventure'.

At the same time, while little detail can be known by
us about heaven, we can know enough. The Bible may
not give us extensive details about its conditions, but it
does tell us some very important things about it.

For one thing, it makes plain that life in heaven will be perfect. There will be no room there for the things that spoil life here—things like sin and suffering, sickness, pain and sorrow—and life will, therefore, be able to blossom into full flower. The epitaph prepared in advance by Benjamin Franklin for his own tombstone gives expression to this very thing: 'The body of Benjamin Franklin, printer, like the cover of an old book, lies here, food for worms; but the work shall not be lost; for it will (as he believes) appear once more in a new and more elegant edition, revised and corrected by its author'.

For another thing, in heaven there will be recognition of one another. We will know our loved ones and be known by them. The Bible gives a number of indications that in heaven there will be both memory and recognition —like Jesus's parable of the Rich Man and Lazarus for example.

This is by no means to suggest that heaven is merely the scene for a resumption of our former life. That is not how it is going to be. We are not going to be clothed with the same old physical make-up—the same flesh, same hair (or lack of it), same teeth (or lack of them), same bodily peculiarities and so on. In heaven we will be different, wonderfully different, because we will be living in a different dimension. And yet we are going to be recognisably the same individuals. Just as the butterfly is breathtakingly different in its beauty and in its freedom of movement from the grub from which it emerged (but at the same time has identity with it), so in heaven we shall be different and yet the same. A kind of metamorphosis. In our case, however, we will be recognisably the same; our friends will know us and we will know them.

I believe all this about heaven. I believe also that part of the joy of heaven will be its work and its worship.

Heaven will not be a state of inactivity. The life to come will be many-sided and it seems clear that one aspect will be service. Heaven will provide opportunities for service of a higher kind, in which all that is best in us, here in this life, will find scope and expression.

There is this, too. It is impossible for us in this life to visualise to any great extent what heaven will be like. But we may be sure that in heaven we will be with Jesus. And I am not forgetting that Jesus is with us now when I say this. I firmly believe that we are in his presence all the time, even in this present world. But our very humanity is a hindrance to our total and constant awareness of his presence, and our sinfulness is a barrier. In heaven we will be free from all shackles and therefore we will be with Jesus as never before.

12

I believe in Hell

YES, I BELIEVE in hell. In other words, I believe that there is an alternative to heaven. I believe that not all people are certain to find their way in the end into heaven; and that there is a real possibility that some may find themselves shut out.

I would be glad to discover that I am wrong in holding this belief. William Barclay used to tell me I was wrong. He believed that the love of God is so great that it can never finally be defeated, and that everyone must finally be won for heaven.

I hope he was right and I am wrong; but I still believe it is the other way round. I believe that God has given us freedom of choice, even to the extent of possibly choosing to refuse his love; and I believe that God, being God, must and will respect that freedom even if it means that we choose hell instead of heaven.

And so I admit that I believe in hell. I say 'admit', which is a word that carries an unmistakable note of apology, because a belief in hell is more than a bit outmoded nowadays and far from popular. I believe in hell, not because I like that belief, nor because I *want* to hold it, but because I feel that I have little option to do otherwise. The Bible, and Jesus in particular, seems to leave me no alternative.

I must make clear that I reject the pictures, once thought by some to be reasonably accurate, which represent hell as a place where evil-doers fry and sinners frizzle. There is an old joke which tells of a Scottish minister of the old school who was preaching one Sunday, as he often did, on the subject of hellfire and damnation, describing in rather grisly detail the tortures of the damned. 'Some of them,' he thundered, 'in that grim day will look up and say plaintively, "But Lord, I didna' ken" and the good Lord will reply, "Well you ken noo".'

Hell is not to be thought of in terms like these. As with heaven, the Bible employs a great deal of imagery with regard to hell which is not intended to be taken literally. The Bible, as a matter of fact, gives considerably less detail about hell than it does even about heaven. It does, however, convey quite clearly that it is real, that it is awful, and that it is to be feared.

The Greek word for hell used in the Bible is *Gehenna* (Γεηεννα). This is derived from a section of the Valley of Hinnom lying just outside the walls of Jerusalem. In early times this was the scene of human sacrifices and later it came to be used by the Jerusalemites, over a very long period, as a vast rubbish dump onto which dead animals were thrown and refuse was burned. Its horrific past reputation, along with the pall of smoke that hung over it continually in these later days, led to *Gehenna* being used as the symbol of the ultimate fate of the godless.

There was a time when the details of the metaphors employed to describe this ultimate future state were taken literally. This sometimes led to preachers graphically outlining the tortures that lay in store for the lost. Nowadays this sort of literal interpretation is largely given up; and, I believe, that is a very good thing.

But I also believe that to abandon the whole idea of hell would be a very bad thing. The Bible seems to me to leave no doubt that hell is real. And so I believe in hell.

If, then, I believe in hell, what do I believe it to be? If it is not a lake of brimstone and fire, how do I describe it? Hell, I believe, is the state or condition of being cut off from God. As heaven might best be described as being in the constant presence of God, face to face, so hell may best be understood as exclusion from that presence. Could any worse fate be imagined, or is any to be more feared?

I believe that hell is real and that hell is terrible; but I do not believe that it is God's desire that anyone should suffer this fate. God does not send anyone to hell. Jesus has made it very plain that God loves us all, even the worst of us; and he would like us all to find our way to heaven. At the same time, since God has given us free-will, he must respect our freedom of choice, even if we should choose against him, and persist in choosing against him to the very end.

In other words, some may find themselves in hell at the end of the day, but if they do, it is because they have chosen to be there and not because God has willed that it should be so. Their judgment has been self-imposed. Jesus came to save, and only to save, not to condemn; but if anyone chooses not to be saved, then inevitably he is choosing to be lost.

But surely God will somehow manage to persuade everyone in the end to accept salvation? Some maintain that he must. It is unthinkable, they say, that God's will can ever ultimately be defeated, even in one single instance. Even if it means wrestling on with some souls beyond the grave, God must surely at the last bring everyone safely home to heaven.

I would like to be able to believe that this is how it will all end; and I hope it may. Nevertheless, as I see it, it can hardly be gainsaid that when God gave mankind free-will, he took the risk of someone saying 'no' to him, and persisting in saying 'no' right to the end. It is, I believe, a real possibility that some may go to hell; but I believe, too, that no one will find himself there who really wants to go to heaven.

In his delightful fantasy, *The Great Divorce,* C S Lewis tells of an excursion from hell to heaven. Anyone may go, anyone at all, and the coach is soon packed full with men and women anxious to escape from the dingy misery that is hell, up to the clear, glad brightness that is heaven.

When they arrive in heaven, their friends who reside there greet them with delight and inform them that they need never return to hell. They are at liberty, if they so decide, to remain in heaven for ever. The visitors from hell are thrilled and delighted; all of them express their intention to stay. But before very long, one after another, they grow tired of heaven and slip away back to the hell they had come from. They find they cannot stand the joys of heaven. The colours are too bright, or the air too pure, or the atmosphere uncongenial. Before even the first day is over, they have all returned to the gloom and the grime of hell.

Lewis's story is, of course, a fantasy. But perhaps it is true to how things are, and to how they are going to be. God has given us free-will. He also gives us his love and he very much wishes us to have eternal life both in this world and in the next. But he accepts that we may say 'no'. No one whom God can persuade to enter in shall be excluded from heaven; but can we be sure that he will ultimately persuade everyone?

I cannot find grounds for absolute certainty that he will; and so I believe in hell.

Conclusion

I END my little book as I began it, with an affirmation of my conviction that belief beats unbelief and beats it hands down. So far as believing in the Christian faith is concerned, it seems to me that it is an open and shut case—*in favour*.

For one thing, the evidence amply justifies belief in the Christian faith on the part of anyone who is prepared to let that evidence speak for itself. Some, it may be, find themselves reluctant to believe because it strikes them as 'too good to be true'. Good—*very good*—it certainly is, but there is much to justify the belief that it is also *true*.

For another thing, belief makes life infinitely more satisfying. Not only because it gives us the promise of a wonderful new life in the next world; but also because it gives new texture and new quality to life in the present.

I am well aware that many people scoff today at believing in the Christian faith; but that is nothing new. They scoffed in New Testament times as well; when the now proud name of 'Christian' was first coined, it was a nickname of derision.

It must be freely admitted (and I hope I have not suggested otherwise in this book) that the Christian faith cannot be proved in any manner akin to a scientific demonstration. But there are, nevertheless, a great many persuasive factors in its favour, some of which have been looked at in the preceding chapters.

What is more, it actually works. It gives an added spice to daily living and is a means of strength in times of crisis.

It works, of course, only if acted upon. Mere acknowledgment that belief has a lot to commend it does not admit anyone to its advantages. There has to be a positive commitment to it.

I used to tell my First Communicants class a story about Blondin, the famous stunt man of the nineteenth century. On one occasion, so the story goes, Blondin had propelled a man in a wheelbarrow on a wire strung across Niagara Falls. In the front row of the large, spellbound crowd was a little boy brought by his father to see the show. When the crossing was completed, Blondin said to the lad, 'Did you enjoy that?'

'Oh, yes!' was the wide-eyed response.

'Do you believe that I could wheel you across the Falls in the barrow?'

Again the lad replied, 'Oh, yes!' What else could he say, he had heard so much of Blondin's prowess beforehand and now he had seen evidence of it with his own eyes?

'Well, then,' the great man continued, 'Climb into the barrow and I will wheel you over to the other side.'

'No thanks,' said the boy, 'I'd rather not.'

He believed that Blondin had the ability to wheel him across in safety, but he was not prepared to stake his life on that belief. In the same way, it is when men and women are prepared to stake their lives—and their souls—on belief in Jesus Christ that he can admit them to the new life he wants them to have.

I once had a long conversation with a successful young businessman on the train from London to Glasgow. The conversation somehow developed into my giving a defence of the Christian faith. The upshot of this was that he freely admitted the cogency of the case I had presented in favour of Christian belief as beyond reasonable doubt.

'But,' he continued, 'It's not for me. I don't need it. I am happy with my present way of life and it has more to offer me, as I see it.' He was, of course, perfectly entitled to adopt that stand-point and make that decision; but he was choosing to miss out on a lot as a result.

It is in the end a matter of values and priorities. My conviction is that belief beats unbelief not only in the sense that the weight of evidence is in its favour, but also in the sense that it has much more of real value to give. I do not mean only heaven—although, if true, as I believe it to be, this is a wonderful thing to have in prospect—but also in the sense of an enriched quality of life and increased usefulness in the here and now.

Let me conclude: It's my belief that having faith in Jesus, and following his Way, is to be strongly and warmly recommended; weighing up the evidence, there is so much to commend it.

Belief certainly does beat unbelief.